John Heydon, Thomas Cross

The Harmony of the World

Being a discourse of God, heaven, angels, stars, planets, earth, the miraculous descentions and ascentions of spirits

John Heydon, Thomas Cross

The Harmony of the World
Being a discourse of God, heaven, angels, stars, planets, earth, the miraculous descentions and ascentions of spirits

ISBN/EAN: 9783337411053

Printed in Europe, USA, Canada, Australia, Japan

Cover: Foto ©Lupo / pixelio.de

More available books at **www.hansebooks.com**

The HARMONY

of the *WORLD*, being a Discourse of God, Heaven, Angels, Stars, Planets, Earth; the miraculous Descentions and Ascentions of Spirits, with the Nature and Harmony of mans Body; the Art of preparing *Rosie Crucian Medicines* to Cure all Diseases. Their Rules to raise bodies decayed, which are verified by a Practical Examination of Principles in the great World.

Whereunto is added, the state of the New Jerusalem, grounded upon the knowledge of Nature, Light of Reason, Phylosophy and Divinity.

All fitted to the Understanding, Use and Profit of Wisdomes Children, and communicated to the sons of Art.

By John Heydon, *Gent.* Φιλονομ⊙ , *a servant of God, and Secretary of Nature.*

And I saw another mighty Angell come down from Heaven, cloathed with a Cloud, and a Rainbow was upon his head, and his face was as it were the Sun, and his feet as Pillers of Fire: And I heard a great voice out of Heaven, saying: behold, the Tabernacle of God is with men, and he will dwell with them, and they shall be his people, and God himself shall be with them, and be their God, *R.v.* 10.1. & 21.3.

LONDON,
Printed for *Robert Horn*, and are to be sold at his shop at the Sign of the *Turks-head* in *Cornhill* neer the Royal Exchange. 1662.

TO THE
Most Honourable, Most Loyall, Magnanimous and High Borne Prince
James Boteler,
Duke of Ormond, *and Lord Lieutenant of his Majesties Kingdome of* Ireland.
Externall, Internall and Eternall Happinesse be Wished.

My Lord,

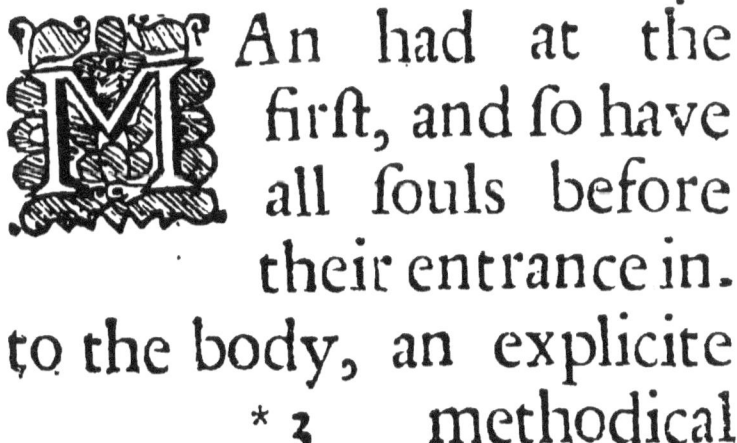An had at the first, and so have all souls before their entrance in-to the body, an explicite methodical

* 3

methodicall knowledge, but they are no sooner vessel'd, but that liberty is lost, and nothing remains but a vast confused notion of the creature; thus had I only a Capacity without power, and a will to do that, which was farr enough above me; in this perplexity I studied severall Arts; for my own sullen fate hath forced me to severall courses of life, but I finde not one hither to to which ends not in Surfets, or satiety, and all the Fortunes of this life are follyes: thus I rameld over all those inventions which the ignorance of men call Sciences; but these endeavours sorting not to my purpose, I Studied then the Seminall forms of things; The Soul of Man, the difference betwixt the Soul of an Angell and an humane Soul, the Nature of God, the Order of Spirits; how they give splendor to the Stars and Planets, how Senfation, Immagination, Reafon and Memory are made, and how the bodyes of Ghofts have as much of folid corporeall fubftance in them as the bodyes of men, what kinde of punifhments the Aerial Officers inflict upon their Malefactours; and how the fpirit of nature is prefent sent every where, and snatcheth into consent the immagination of the mother, which forcibly reteyns the note, and will be sure to seale it on the body of the Infant, for what rude inchoation the soul of the World has begun in the matter of the Fætus, this signature is comprehended in the whole designe, and afterwards compleated by the presence and operation of the

the particular soul of the Infant. After I knew what the soul was before it came into the body: I found presently what it was in the flesh; then all I desired was but to keep my body in health, and this being obteyned: I went yet further, *To see what would become of the Genii, when the firing of the World has done due execution upon that unfortunate crue, and tedious and*

and direfull torture has wearied their afflicted Ghosts that are earthly, into an utter recesse from all matter, and thereby into a profound sleep or death; that after a long series of years, when not only the fury of the fire is utterly slaked, but that vast Atmosphere of Smoke & Vapours, which was sent up during the time of the Earths conflagration, has returned back in Copious Showers

of

of *Raine* which will again make *Seas* and *Rivers*, will bind and consolidate the ground; and falling exceeding plentifully all over, make the soyle pleasant and fruitfull and the *Aire* coole and wholsome, that Nature recovering thus to her advantage, and becomming youthfull again, and full of genital *Salt* & moisture, the souls of all living creatures belonging to these lower Regions of the Earth and Aire

Aire, will awaken orderly in their proper places, the Seas and Rivers will be again replenished with fish; the Earth will send forth all manner of fowles, foure footed beasts, creeping things; & the Souls of men also shall then catch life from the more pure and Balsamick parts of the Earth, and be cloathed again in terrestriall bodies; and lastly the Aeriall Genii, that Element becoming again wholsome

some and vitall, shall in due order and time, awaken and revive in the cool rorid Aire, which expergefaction into life is accompanied say they, with propensions answerable to those resolutions they made with themselves in those fiery torments, & with which they fell into their long sleep, this is the primative truth of the Creation, the Antient, real Phylosophy of the Hebrews and Egyptians, But new Philosophy

Dedicatory.

sophy to our common Scribers, and I propose it not for your instruction, Nature hath already inriched you with Learning, judgment and Candor, and I would make you my Patron not my Pupill; if therefore amongst your serious and more deare retirements, you can allow this Edilis but some few Minutes, and think them not lost, you will perfect

fect my Ambition, that is to present my self,

November, 12th.   *My Lord*
1661.

Your Honours most

humble Servant,

John Heydon.

The Preface.

IN Mr. *Slades* Orchard at *Sidmouth* in *Devon*, about the dawning or *day-break*, being tyred with a tedious solitude, and those pensive thoughts which attend it, after much losse and more labour, I suddenly fell asleep; Here then *day* was no sooner born then strangled: I was reduced to a *night* of more deep Tincture than that which I had formerly spent: My *fancy* placed me in a *Region* of inexpressable obscurity, and as I thought more than Natural, but without any terrours; I was in a firm even temper, and though without incouragements, not onely resolute, but well pleased: I moved every way for discoveries, but was still entertained with darknesse and silence; and I thought my self translated

lated to the *land of Deſſolation*. Being thus troubled to no purpoſe, and wearied with long endeavours, I reſolv'd to reſt my ſelf; and ſeeing I could finde nothing I expected, if any thing could finde me. I had not long continued in this humour; but I could here the whiſpers of a ſoft winde, that travell'd towards me; and ſuddenly it was in the leaves of the Trees, ſo that I concluded my ſelf upon the ſouth-ſide *Hewill* upon *Hazle-hill* in *Warwick-ſhire*, among the ſhady walks of thoſe woods, wherein often by the River ſide, & by the Chriſtal fountain, having loſt the ſight of the reſt of the world, and the world of me; I found out in that hidden ſolitude very excellent experiments in Medicines, admirable glorious tinctures, and Teleſmes in the *Earth*, and the ſecrets of Nature, *&c.* with this breath came the *day-light*, and with it ſuch a *bright flame*, that it ſeemed to exceed that of the *Sun*: After we had done our holy things at the twentieth houre

The Preface.

houre of the tenth day of *June* 1648. there appeared to us, after their ufuall manner; *Seven men cloathed in filk garments, with Cloaks after the* Englifh *mode, with purple Stockins, and Crimfon Velvet Coats, red and fhining on their Breaft : nor were they all thus clad, but onely two of them, who were the chief :* On *the ruddier and taller of thefe two, other two waited, but the leffe and paler had three attendants:* So that they made up feven in all; they were about forty years of Age, but lookt as if they had not reacht thirty; when they were asked who they were? They anfwered, that they were *Homines Aerii, Aerial men,* who are born and dye as we; but that their life is much longer then ours, as reaching to three hundred years, and they raife each other from death to life. Being asked concerning the Immortality of *Dæmons* ? They anfwered ; *Nihil quod cuique proprium effet fupereffe;* that they were of a nearer affinity with the *Divi* then we: but yet infinitely dif-
ā 2   ferent

ferent from them: and that their happinesse or misery, as much transcended ours, as ours does the bruit Beasts; that they knew all things, past, present, or to come, and what is hid, whether Moneyes or Books; and that the lowest sort of them, were the *Genii* of the best and noblest men amongst the *Rosie Crucians*, as the basest men are the trainers up of the best sort of dogs; that the tenuity of their bodies was such, that they can neither do us good nor hurt; saving in what they may be able to doe by *spectres* and *terrers*, and impartent of *knowledge*, we asked what Religion was best amongst us? they answered the *Protestant*; and *Episcopacy* was the best *Form of Church Government*, and that they were both publick professors in an *Accademy*, and that he of the lesser stature had three hundred D*isciples*, the other twenty: we asked further, why they would not reveale such treasures as they knew unto men? They answered, that there

The Preface.

there was a speciall Law against it, upon a very grevious penalty.

These *Aireyall Inhabitants*, stayd at least ten hours disputing and arguing of sundry things, amongst which, one was *the Originall of the World* : *The Taller denying that God made the World, ab æterno:* The Lesser affirmed that he so created it every moment, that if heshould desist but one moment it would perish, *whereupon the other cited some things out of the disputations of R.C. Electione fraternitatis caput;* in *the Rosie Crucian Axiomata, the second Book:* which books, if this be acceptable, I shall shortly publish: and the *Rota*, *The Wise mans Crown*; The second Book of *Rosie Crucian* Physick, and *The Temple of Wisdome*. The Book of *Geomancy*, *Astrology* and *Telesmes*; And named severall other Treatises, part whereof I know, part not, which were of the *Rosie Crucians* Writings, and withall did openly professe himself of the Reverend Order.

The Preface.

As these went away from us, there came a most Heavenly Odorous Aire, like that of sweet Bryers, but not so full and ranke; in this admiration were we conveyed I know not how, into the Orchard again; where this Perfume being blown over, there succeeded a pleasant humming of Bees, amongst Flowers, Herbs and Leaves that were there, and this did somewhat discompose me, for I Judged it not suitable with the complexion of the place, which was now again darke and like midnight, then was I somewhat troubled, with these unexpected occurrences; When a new appearance diverted my apprehensions. Not farr off on my right hand, I could discover a white weake light, not so cleere as that of a candle, but misty and much resembling an Atmosphere, towards the centers it was of *Purple colour* like the *Elesian sun-shine*, but in the Dilatation of the circumference Milky: And if we consider the joynt Tincture of
the

The Preface.

the parts, it was a *painted Vesper*, a figure of that splendour which the old *Romans* called *Sol mortilorum*; whilest I admired this strange scæne, there appeared in the middle of the *purple colours*, a sudden commotion, and out of their *very centre* did sprout a *certain flowery light*, as it were the *flame* of a Taper, very *bright* it was, sparkling and twinckling like the day-Star; the beams of this new Planet issuing forth in smal skeins and rivilets, lookt like threds of silver, which being reflected against the Trees, discovered a curious green Umbrage; and I found my self in that Mathematical Grove of conspiring Apple Trees, &c. set by Master *William Slade*; Under this shade and skreen, did lodge a number of Nitingales, Thrushes, and Owsels or Black-birds, which first I discovered by their whitish breasts; These peeping through their leavy Cabinets, rejoyced at this strange light, and having first plum'd themselves, stirr'd the still aire with their

Musick

The Preface.

Mufick; thefe (with many other little birds that ftreined their pretty throats) which I thought was very pretty, for the filence of the night, fuiting with the folitude of the place, made me judge it heavenly: The ground both neer and far off, prefented a pleafing kinde of Checquer; for this new *Star* meeting with fome drops of dew, made a multitude of bright refractions, as if the earth had been paved with Diamonds. Thefe rare and various accidents kept my Soule bufied, but to interrupt my thoughts, as if it had been unlawfull to examine what I had feen; another more admirable Object interpofed, I could fee between me and the light, a moft exquifite *Divine Beauty*, black and lovely, her frame neither long nor fhort, but a mean decent ftature; *Attyred fhe was* (according to the moft *Curious mode of the Country*, at *Sydmouth* in the *County of Devone* near *Exeter*,) In a habit beft pleafed her own nature, *for fhe valued not*

The Preface.

not Vanity; her *Eyes* were quick, fresh and *Celestiall*, but had something of a Start, as if she had been puzzled with a suddain occurrence, her Countenance was Amiable; from her black vaile, did her features break forth, like Sun Beams in a mist, her haire ran dishevelled to her breasts, and returned to her cheeks in curles, and that hayre behind was rowled to a curious Globe, with a smal short spire Flowered with *Purple* and *Skie* coloured *Knotts*, her *Rings* were pure entyre *Embralds*, for she valued no Mettals, and her *Pendants* of burning *Carbuncles*; To be short, her whole habit was *Youth-full* and *Flowry*, of *Skie Coloured Silk*, thin and loose, *Fancied with Violet, Silver, White, Blew, Green and Scarlet Ribbands*; which lookt very fine and pleasant in a Golden Morning, and smelt like the East and was throughly aired with rich *Arabian Diapasms*. But whilst I admired her perfections, and prepared to make my addresses, *she prevents me with a voluntary ry approach.* Here indeed I expected some discourse from her, but she looking very seriously and silently in my face *takes me by the hand,* and I thought it not amisse to walk with so sweet a *Lady,* when she so fairely invited me; now the *Light* which I had formerly admired, proved to be her *Attendant :* for it moved like an usher before her. This service added much to her Glory, and it was my only care to observe her, who though she wandered not; Yet verily she followed no known path. Her walke was Green, being Furred with a fine small Grasse, which felt like Plush, for it was very soft; and purled all the way with *Dasies, Primroses, Violets, Honeysuckles,* and *sweet flowers*; when we came out of this our *Arborel* or *Courtly Orchard* of *Apple Trees*; I could perceive a strange clearnesse in the *Aire,* not like that of *Day*; neither can I affirm it was *night*; the Stars indeed perched over us, and stood glimmering, as it were on the tops

of

The Preace.

of high hills; for we were in a most deep bottome, betwixt *Corle* and *Bulverton*, and the *earth* over lookt us; so we walked over a little *Rivolet*, through *my Fathers first, second and third Courts*, and passed the last gate, that directs to a *bridge*, which we went over; and we had not gone very far, when I had a great desire to hear my *Mistrisse* speak, (for so I judged her now) that if possible, I might receive some information from her: how to bring this about, I did not well know; For she seem'd very coy, rough and averse from discourse, but having resolv'd with my self to disturb her. I asked if she would favour me with her Name? To which she replyed very familiarly, as if she had known me long before, My true and faithfull Servant (said she) my Name is *Beata*; you do here behold, *The Harmony of the World, Man, the Soul, Nature* and *Religion*, and had it been your fortune barely to know the secrets of *Nature, Reason* and *Philosophy,*

phy, with all the sweet circumstances of them, which few upon Earth understand, I would not have been your *Mistris:* and now my dearly beloved Servant J.H. publish this *Rosie Crucian* mistery, and add it to your former discourses, *viz. The Temple of Wisdome, The Rosie Crucian infallible Axiomata:* Your new Method *Of Rosie Crucian* Physick and Medicines, *for long life, Health, Youth, Wisdome and Vertue, and to alter, change and amend the state of the body;* And if the rude Readers be so wise they cannot understand you; leave the discovery to God, who when it is his blessed will, can instruct the better sort of them; I charge you upon pain of loosing my Love, teach no man, what you have from me, unlesse you finde them of your own disposition, its truth the World looks for Dreams and Revelations, as the Train to their invisible Righteousnesse; but you shall deliver what I send to the Sons of Art (for so I call those whose Qualities are as yours) let

the

The Preface.

them know by the *Rosie Crucian M* that there are but two *Elements, Earth and VVater,* Air is the Cæment of two worlds and a Medly of Extreams. It is natures common place, her index, where you may finde all that ever she did or intends to do; This is the Worlds *Rendezvous*; in this are innumerable *Idea's* of Men, Beasts, Fish and Foul, Trees, Herbs, and all creeping things, this is *Mare Rerum invisibilium,* for all the conceptions *in sinu superioris naturæ,* wrap themselves in this Tiffany, before they imbarke in the shell. It retayns the species of all things whatsoever, and is the immediate receptacle of spirits, after dissolution, whence they passe to the Æthereal Region, which is a most silent Fire. This Fire passeth through all things in the world, and it is natures Chariot, in this she rides; when she moves this moves, and when she stands this stands, like the Wheels in *Ezekiel,* whose Motion dependeth on that of the spirit, this is the

Mask

The Preface.

Mask and Screen of the Almighty, wheresoever he is, this *Train* of *Fire* attends him. Thus he appears to *Moses* in the *Bush*, but it was in Fire; the Prophet sees him break out at the *North*, but like a *Fire* catching it self; at *Horeb* he is attended with a *mighty strong wind* rending the Rocks in pieces, but after this comes the *Fire*, and with it a still small voice, *Esdras* also defines a God, whose service is conversant in *VVinde* and *Fire*; this face is the vestment of the *Divine Majesty*, his back parts which he shewed to *Moses*, but his naked royall Essence none can see and live; The Glory of his presence would swallow up the naturall man, and make him altogether spiritual, thus *Moses* his face after conference with him shines, and from his smal *Tincture* you may guess at you future estate in the regeneration, for to know nothing is life eternal, because all invisibles came out of the invisible

ble God, & this is *The way to bliss*; when you come to the *Chaos* you shall find it *blood red*, becaufe the Central Sulphur prefents it fo; in your preparation it is white like *Quick-filver*, & tranfparent like the Heavens, & before the fall of man, there was a more plentifull and large Communion between *Heaven* and *Earth*, *God* and the *Elements*, than there is now in your days upon mans tranfgreffion ; *Malcuth* was cut off from the *Han*, fo that a breach was made between both worlds, and their Chanel of *Influences* difcontinued. Now *Malcuth* is the invifible *Archetypal Moon*, by which your vifible *Cæleftial Moon* is governed, and impregnated, and *God* to punifh the fin of *Adam*, withdrew himfelf from the creatures; fo that they were not feafted with the fame meafure of influences as formerly. But the Angels became Minifters of the *Gofpel*, and the *Law* was in their hands, till *Chrift* fhould take it into his own, and *Raziel* the Angel was prefently difpatched to communicate

nicate the intelligence to *Adam* & to acquaint him with the *Harmony of the Gods*, & their *Divine Idea's*, *Angels* & their *Genii*, *Spheres* and their *Spirits*, *Stars*, *Planets* and their *Souls* or naturall *Ideas*, *Men* and their *Guardians*, and how by the influence of the *Starrs* these visible creaturs receive Vertue, Life, Knowledg, Sense and Motion; and God when the matter was prepared by love, for light, gives out his *fait Lux*, which was no *Creation* as most think, but an *Emanation* of the *World* in whom was *life*, and that life is the light of men, this is that light Saint *John* speaks of, *that it shines in the darknesse, and the darknesse comprehended it not*. No sooner had this Divine Light pierced the bosome of the matter, but the *Idea* of the whole material world appeared in those primitive waters like an image in a Glasse: By this *Idea* it was that the *Holy Ghost* framed and modled the universall structure, This R. C. mistery of the Idea is excellently manifested

The Preface.

ted in the Magicall Analyfis of bodies: For he that knows how to immitate the protochimiftry of the Spirit, by feparation of the principles, wherein the life is imprifoned, may fee the impreffe of it experimentally in the outward naturall veftiments: when the Unity of the Trinity had applyed themfelves to the matter, there was extracted from the bofome of it a *thin fpirituall celeftial fubftance* wch receiving a tincture of heat & light proceeding from the divine Treafuries, became a pure fincere innoxious fire, of this the *Bodyes of Angels Confift*, as alfo the *Empyreall Heaven*, where intellectuall effences have their refidence: this extract being thus fetled above, and feparated from the Maffe, retaynd in it a vaft portion of light, and made the firft day without a *Sun*, but the fplendour of the word expelling the darknefs downwards, it became more fetled, and compact towards the centre, and made a horrible

rible thick night; and thus *God* was between the *light* and *darknesse*, for the spirit remained still on the face of the interiour portion, to extract more from it: in the second separation was reduced *Aier Agilis*, a spirit not so refined as the former, but vitall; and in the next degree to it, this was extracted in such abundance, that it filled all the space from the Mass to the *Empyreall heaven*, under which it was condenced to a water, but of a different constitution from the *Elemental*; and this is the body of the *inter-stellar skie*, the inferiour portion of this second extract from the *moon* to the *earth* remained *Aire*, still partly to divide the *inferiour and superiour Waters*; but chiefly for the respiration and nourishment of the creatures, and this is that which is properly called the *Firmament*; *And* on the second day *God Created the Spirit of the Firmament*, and in the outward *Geometricall Composure* it answers to *Natura media*, for it is spread through all things, hinders vacuity and keeps all
the

The Preface.

the parts of nature in a firme invisible union; Nothing now remains but the two inferiour principles, *Earth* and *Water*; the Earth was an impure sulphurous substance, or *Caput mortuum*, of the Creation the *Water* also was phlegmatick, cold and raw, not so vitall as the former extractions, but the *Divine Spirit* to make his work perfect moving also upon these, imparted to them life and heat, and made them fit for future productions; the earth was so over cast, and mantled with the water, that no part thereof was to be seen, but the spirit orders a retreat, that it may be expofed to the *Cælestiall influences*, the light as yet was not confined, but retayning his vast flux and primitive liberty, equally posseft the whole creature. On the fourth day it was collected to a *Sun*, and taught to know his Fountaine; the darknesse whence proceed the corruptions, and consequently the death of the creature, was imprisoned in the *Centre*, but breaks out still when the day gives it leave: and you must

The Preface.

must know every *Element* is threefold, for example, there is a threefold earth: First, there is *Terra Elementaris*: then there is *Terra Cælestis*, and lastly *Terra Spiritualis*, the influences of the spiritual earth by mediation of the Celestial, are united to the terrestrial, & are the cause of life, &c. These three are the fundamentalls of art and nature, the first answers to *God the Father*, being the natural foundation of the creature: the second principle is the infallible Magnet, the Mistery of Union, by this all things may be attracted whether Phisicall or metaphisical, be the distance never so great, this is *Jacabs Ladder* without this, there is no ascent, or descent either influentiall or personall, this answers *to God the Son*, for it is that which mediates between extreams, and makes *inferiours* and superiours communicate: the third Principle is not *ex quo*, but *per quod omnia*, this can do all in all, and the faculties thereof, I may not tell you; it an-

swers

The Preface.

fwers to the *Holy Ghost*, and amongſt naturalls it is the only Agent and Artificer, *&c.* and by theſe you may performe miraculous things; for there is not a compound in all nature, but hath in it a little *Sun* and a little *Moon*, and what offices foever the two greatLuminaries perform for the conſervation of the great world in generall, theſe two little Luminaries performe the like for the conſervation of their Microcoſme in particular; the *Sun* and *Moon* are two principles, the one active, the other *paſſive*, this maſculine that fæminine, they have Spirits and Angels attending them as all bodies have, and the Starrs likewiſe have ſpirits that carry influence to one another and to the Earth, *&c.*

And as the great world conſiſts of three parts, the Elementall, the Cæleſtiall and the Spirituall, above all which God himſelf is ſeated in that infinite inacceſſible light, which ſtreams from his own nature, even ſo Man hath in him his *Earthly Elementarll*

The Preface.

mentall parts, together with the *Celestiall and Angelicall natures*; in the Centre of all which moves, and shines the *Divine Spirit*, the Sensuall, Cæleſtial, Ætherial part of man, is that whereby we do move, see, feel, taſt and smell, and have a Commerce with all materiall objects whatsoever, it is the same in us as in Beaſts, and it is derived from Heaven, where it is predominant to all the inferiour Earthly creatures, it is *Anima Mundi*, vulgarly called by *Aſtrologers*, *Anima Media*, becauſe the influences of the Divine Nature are conveyed through it to the more materiall parts of the creature, with which of themſelves they have no proportion; by means of this *anima media*, or the ætheriall Nature, man is made subject to the *influence of Stars*, and is diſpoſed of, partly by the *Cæleſtiall Harmony*; for this middle spirit is of a fruitfull inſinuating nature, and carryes such a ſtrange deſire to multiply it ſelf, that the Cæleſtiall forme ſtirs up, and excites

the

the Elementall; as is manifest in those Herbs which open at the rising, and shut towards the Sun set, which motion is caused by the Spirit being sensible of the approach and departure of the Sun, for indeed the flowers are as it were the spring of the spirit, where it breaks forth and streams, as it appears by the sweet smells that are most cælestiall, and comfortable there. Again this is more evident in the plantanimalls, as the vegetable Lamb, the Arbor *Casia*, and severall others; but this will not sink with any, but such as have seen this spirit separated from his elements, *where I leave it for this time*: Next, to this sensuall nature of man, is the Angelical, or Rationall spirit, this spirit adheres somtimes to the *mens* or superiour portion of the soul, & then it is filled with the Divine light; but most commonly it descends into the æthereal, inferior portion, which Saint *Paul* calls *Homo Animalis*, where it is altered by the *Cælestiall influences*, and diversly

versly distracted with the irregular *affections* and passions of the sensuall nature, above the rationall spirit is the *mens*, commonly called *spiraculum vitarum*; this is that spirit which God breathed into man, and by which man is united again to God; Hence there is in nature a certain spirit which applyes himself to the matter, and Actuates in every generation. That there is also a passive intrinsecall principle, where he is more immediately resident then in the rest, and by mediation of which, he communicates with the more grosse materiall parts, for there is in nature a certain chaine or subordinate propinquity of complexions between visibles and invisibles, and this is it by which the superiour, spirituall essenses descend, and converse here below with the matter: do not mistake me Gentlemen, I speak not in this place of the Divine spirit, but I speak of a certain Art by which a particular spirit may be united to the universall, and nature by consequence

consequence may be strangely exalted and multiplyed. Now then in every frame there are three leading principles, the first is this *Anima* aforesaid, the second is called *spiritus mundi*, and this spirit is the medium *per quod anima infunditur & movet suum Corpus*: The third is a certain Oleus ætherial water: This is *Menstrum* and *Matrix Mundi*, for in it all things are framed and preserved, as soon as the passive spirit attracts the *Anima*, which is done when the first link in the chaine moves, then the ætheriall water in a moment attracts the passive spirit, for this is the first visible receptacle wherein the superiour natures are concentrated, and this passive spirit is a thin Aireal substance, the only immediate vestiment wherein the *Anima* wraps her self, when she descends and applyes to generation; the radicall vitall liquor, is a pure cælestiall nature, answering in proportion and complexion to the superiour *interstellar waters*, the *Soul* being thus

The Preface.

thus confined, by lawfull *Magick*, in this liquid Chriftall, the light which is in her ftreams through the water, and then it is *Lux manifefté vifibilis ad occulum*, in which ftate it is firft made fubject to the Artift: here now lyes the miftery of the R. C. his moft fecret and miraculous pyramid, whofe firft Unity or Cone is alwayes in *Horizonte Eternitatis*, but his Bafis or quadrate is here below in *Horizonte Temporis*, the *Anima* confifts of three portions of light, and one of the matter: the Paffive fpirit hath two parts of the matter and two of the light; wherefore it is called *Natura Media*, and *Sphæra equalitatis*, the Cæleftial water hath but one portion of light to three of the matter. Now the chain of defcent which concernes the fpiritual parts, is grounded on a fimilitude or Symbol of Nature; and there being but three portions of light in the *Anima*, and two in the paffive fpirit, the inferiour attracts the fuperiour; then there being but one portion

The Preface.

portion in the cæleſtiall nature, and two in the middle ſpirit; this ſolitary ſhining unity attracts the other *Binarious*, to fortifie and augment its ſelf, as light joynes with light or flame with flame; and thus they hang in a vitall magneticall ſeries. Againe the chain of aſcent which concerns the matter is performed thus: The *Cæleſtial* nature differs not in ſubſtance from the *Aireal Spirit*, but only in degree and complexion, and the *Aireal Spirit* differs from the materiall part of the ſoul in conſtitution only, and not in nature: ſo that theſe three being but one ſubſtantially, may admit of a perfect Hypoſtaticall Union, and be carried by a certaine intellectuall light in *Horizontem Mundi ſuper ſupremi*, and ſo ſwallowed up of immortallity: thus have I ſhewed you what you deſire, *viz. The Harmony of the World*, how the ſoul deſcends and aſcends to the body, what the ſoul of the World is, and what the ſoul of the Earth, and how the *Primum mobile* ſets all a going, you know now

The Preface.

now the universall spirit of nature, & his strange abstruce miraculous ascent & descent. I shall speak one word more of man & his state after death, and this will prove not a Preface only, but an introduction or a key to the following discourse, & the secrets of nature even frō God downward.

And now what I speak of the dissolution of man shall be very brief, because I will close up my discourse, as he doth his life with death, death is *recessus vitæ in Absconditum:* not the annihilation of any one principle, but a retreat of hidden natures to the same state they were in, before they were manifested, this is occasioned by the disproportion and inequality of the matter: for when the *Harmony* is broken by the excesse of any one Principle, the vital twist (without a timely reduction of the first vnity) disbands and unravells. In this recesse the severall ingredients of man returne to those severall Elements, from whence they came at first, in their accesse to a
compound

The Preface.

compound: thus the earthly parts, as we fee by experience, returne to the earth, the Cæleſtiall to a ſuperiour Heavenly Lymbus, and the ſpirit to God that gave it: and the breathing of it into *Adam*, proves it proceeded from *God*; and *therefore the ſpirit of God* : Thus *Chriſt breathed on his Apoſtles, and they received the Holy Ghoſt : In* Ezekiel, *The ſpirit comes from the foure windes, and breathes upon the ſlain, that they might live.* Now this ſpirit was a ſpirit of life, the ſame with that breath of life, which was breathed into the firſt man, and he became a living ſoul; but without doubt, the breath or ſpirit of life *is the ſpirit of God :* Neither is this ſpirit in man alone, but in all the great world, though after another manner; *For God breathes continually,* and paſſeth through all things like an *aire* that refreſheth; Hence it is that *God* in Scripture hath ſeveral names, now at the diſſolution, the principles of man, part, as ſometimes friends doe ſeveral wayes,

The Preface.

wayes, *Earth* to *Earth,* and *Heaven* to *heaven*; but the part which is the *Astrall man* hovers sometimes about the *dormitories* of the Dead, and that because of the *Magnetisme* or sympathy, which is between him and the radical vitall moisture: In this *Idolnm* is the seat of imagination, and it retains after death an impresse of those Passions and Affections, to which it was subject in the Body: this makes him haunt these places, where the whole man hath been most conversant, and imitate the Actions and Gestures of this life: This Magnetisme is excellently confirmed by that *Apparition* in *Southwark*, so familiarly seen at *noon-day*, answering *questions, &c.* But this scœn exceeds not the Circuit of one year; for when the body begins fully to corrupt, the spirit returns to his original Element: I am now to speak of man as he is subject to a supernatural judgement; and to be short, my Sentinent is this. I conceive there are besides the *Emperial Heaven,*

The Preface.

Heaven, two inferiour Manſions or Receptacles of Spirits. The one is that, which our Saviour cals σκότῶ ἐξότερον, and this is it whence there is no Redemption: ὅθεν ὥστε ἀκβαινυσιν, *unde animæ nunquam egrediuntur:* The other I ſuppoſe, is anſwerable to the Elyſian fields, ſome delicate, pleaſant Region, the Suburbs of Heaven: Thoſe ſeven mighty mountains, whereupon grow Roſes and Gillyflowers, *&c.* Many believe there is a ſucceſſive gradual aſcent of the Soul, according to the proceſſe of expiation; and they make her inter-reſidence in the *Moon;* but let it be where it will, my opinion is, that this middlemoſt manſion is appointed for ſuch ſouls, whoſe whole man hath not perfectly repented in this world: But notwithſtanding, they are *de ſalvandorum numero*, and reſerved in this place, to further Repentance in the ſpirit, for thoſe offences they committed in the Fleſh. I doe not here maintain that *Ignis fatuus* of *Purgatory*, or any

ſuch

such painted immaginary *Tophet*, but that which I speak of (if I am not much mistaken) I have a strong scripture, for it is that of Saint Peter, where he speaks of *Christ* being put to death in the flesh, but quickned by the spirit: By which also he went, and preached unto the spirits that were in Prison: which sometimes were disobedient, when once the long suffering of *God* waited in the dayes of *Noah*, while the Arke was a preparing, wherein few, that is, eight souls were saved by water. These spirits were the souls of those who perished in the Flood; and were reserved in this place till *Christ* should come, and preach repentance to them, and it is not said that the spirit it self precisely preached unto them; but he who went thither by the spirit, namely *Christ*, in the Hypostaticall Union of His Soul and God-head, which Union was not before the Flood, when these dead did live: again, it is said that he preached unto spirits, not to men: to those

The Preface.

hose which were in prison, not to those which were *in vivis*, and this you may read at large in my *Idea of the Law*, &c. and the Apostle confirms it in another place, Chap. 4. *verf.*6. νεκροῖς εὐηγγελίσθη, the dead were preached to, not the living, and these spirits were sometimes disobedient, in the days of *Noah*, whence I gather they were disobedient at the time of preaching, and this is plain out of the subsequent Chapter, *For this cause was the Gospel preached also to them that are dead, that they might be judged according to men in the flesh, but live according to God in the spirit*: Now this Judgment in the flesh was grounded on their disobedience in the days of *Noah*, for which also they were drowned, but Salvation according to *God* in the spirit proceeded from their repentance at the preaching of *Christ* which was after *death*; I do not conceive there shall be a Resurrection of every Species; but rather their Terrestrial parts together with the Element of water

water, (for there shall be no more Sea) shall be united in one mixture with the Earth, and fixed to a pure Diaphanous substance, this is Saint *Johns Christall Gold*, a fundamentall of the new *Jerusalem* so called, not in the respect of colours but constitution, their spirits at last shall be reduced to their first Lymbus, a sphere of pure ætheriall fire like rich ætheriall Tapestry spread under the *Throne of God:* Neither do I impose this on the Reader, as if I sat in the infalible chaire, but I am confident the Text of it self will speak no other sense; as for the Doctrine it is no way hurtfull, but in my opinion as it detracts not from the mercy of God, so it adds much to the comfort of man; These were her instructions which were no sooner delivered, but she gave me a book curiously wrought and garnished with flourishing *Figures of Golden Hyeroglyphicks*, with Azure and Silver Letters, saying, I give you leave to be free to those you finde of your own nature, and to

publish

The Preface.

publish your works you have written, viz. *The Temple of Wisdome*, and your Treatise of Chymical Medicines, *Aurum Potabile, Ignis vitæ, Stella vitæ, Nutrix vitæ, Radix vitæ, Amicus vitæ, Vis vitæ, Adjutrix, vitæ, Succus vitæ, Sanguis vitæ, Lac vitæ, Nutrix vitæ, Filius Solis Cælestis Salus vitæ, Filia Lunæ Cælestis, Medulla vitæ Arabick Diapasmes, Deliciæ vitæ, Anima Solis,* Approved by large experience to be effectuall in supplying mans continuall waste and expence of spirit and preservatives against infection, melancholy and all decayes in nature, and I would have you let the poor sick people have your Oyle of Gold, Spirits of Hony, of Lemons, Oranges, Saffron, Cinamon, Cloves, Angelica, Clary, Bawme, Rosemary, Wormwood, Mace, Nutmegges, Mint, Pantarva, to cure them of their diseases for a sickly time is comming; cure all that comes to you. I know they will reward you evill for good, and hatred for your good will; but it is pitty that

The Preface.

many thousands will dye for want of your Medicines, I know you are of a Noble nature, and faithfull to falshearted men; you are free and gentle of spirit, but my dearly beloved *J. H.* you must not in your publick writings exceed my allowance, I am your love, and you must not let every man that Petitions you see my face for I am a Virgin and a Mother of Children, yet never was I lookt upon with adulterate eyes: And now I am going to the invisible Region let not that proverbe take place with you, out of sight, out of minde; remember me and be happy: Then she brought me to a clear large light, and then I returned her book, and here she shewed me those things I must not speak off: when we were past the Rock of the River on the East side of the house, she walked up the Hill from the deep vale of flowers and Primeroses to the face of the plain where her clew of Sun-beams, her light that went before her waited upon her, here

Beata

The Preface.

Beata stopt in a mute ceremony, for I was to be left alone, she look't upon me in silent smiles mixt with a pretty kind of sadnesse, for we were unwilling to part, but her hour of translation was come, and taking her leave, she past before my eyes into the Æther of Nature, and this was my Mistris, it is Nature for I have no other, I leave fine Ladies to fine Ladds, and speak of my *Beata* or *Naturæ*; for so she is called, &c.

IT *was scarce* day, *when all alone*
I saw Beata *and her Throne*
In flesh, Azure Damases *she was drest,*
And o're a Saphire Globe *did rest;*
This slipperie Sphære when I did see
Fortune, *I thought it had been thee:*
But when I saw she did present
A Majesty *more* Permanent,
I thought my cares not lost, if I
Should finish my discovery.
    Sleepie she look'd to my first sight;
As if she had watched *all the night*
And underneath her hand was spread,
The White Supportor *of her head:*
But at my second studied View,
I could perceive a silent Dew

The Preface.

Steale down her Cheeks, *leaſt it ſhould ſtain*
Thoſe Cheeks *where onely ſmiles ſhould* raigne.
The tears ſtream'd down for haſt, and all
In chaines of liquid pearle *did fall*
Faire ſorrows, and more deare than joyes,
Which are but empty Ayres and Noyſe:
Your drops *preſent a richer prize,*
For they are ſomething like her Eyes.
   Pretty white foole! why haſt thou been
Sulli'd with Tears, and not with Sin
'Tis true : Thy teares, like poliſh't skies
Are the bright Roſials *of thy* Eyes,
But ſuch ſtrange Fates *doe noe attend*
As if thy woes would never end :
From Drops *to ſighs they turn, and then*
Thoſe ſighs returne to drops *agen,*
But while the ſilver Torent ſeeks
Thoſe flowers that watch it in thy cheeks,
The White and Red *Beata* wears
Turne to Roſe-water *all her tears*
   Have you beheld a Flame, *that ſprings*
From incenſe, *when ſweet curled, rings*
Of ſmoak attend her laſt weak fires
And ſhe all in perfumes *expires*
So dy'd Beata ; *Here ſaid ſhe*
Let not this Vial *part from thee :*
It holds my heart, *though now 'tis ſpill'd,*
And into waters all diſtill'd

'Tis

The Preface.

'Tis constant still : Trust not false smiles
Who smiles, and weeps not she beguiles
Nay trust not tears : false are the few
Those tears are many that are true ;
Trust me and take the better choice
Who hath my tears, can want no Joyes.

I shall now speak a word more concerning my self, & another concerning the *Common Artist*, and then I have done, it will be questioned perhaps what I am, & especially what my Religion is? Take this short Answer; *I am neither Papist nor Sectary, but a true resolute Protestant in the best sense of the Church of England;* Geomancy, Astrology, Philosophy, Phisick, the Law and Presbytery are all imperfect, and a meer mixture of fancies and inconsistent contrary principles, which no way agree with the *Harmony and method of God and Nature.*

The huge Volums (*of Law, Anabaptism* &c. *Phylosophy, Astrology, Chymistry, Phisick and Geomancy,* &c. like the *Oxe* roasted in Saint *Bartholomew Faire* do proclame
plenty

The Preface.

plenty of Labour and invention, but afford little, that is wholesome, sound and good.

Some *Learned Gentlemen* have desired me to give the world a satisfactory Character of *William Lilly*, I know not what to say more then all men know, *He was a Labourer or Ditchers Son, by education a Taylor; brought up by one* Paylen *in the Strand*.

I come to prove it by Art.

William Lilly in his Introductional Nativity Example, gives the ☽ being in 1. 44. ♊ and under the first Circle 40. 74. 16. oblique Descention, which is conspiciously false, and I prove it thus,

Longit. ☽.	1. 44. ♊.
Latit. North.	5. 0.
Decl. Sept. sub terra	25. 29.
Ascentio Recta	58. 30
Ascentio Recta I.C.	42. 10.
Dist. à I.C.	16. 20.
Circle.	40.
Descentio Obliqua	82. 4.

Ergo

The Preface.

Ergo, *Lilly* is distant from the truth herein, no less then eight whole degrees, and forty minites, which by consequence proves all his directions of the Moon to her Promittors, full nine years false, and upwards by *Naylods* measure of time.

In this Vernall figure, 1661. (where we thought he would have been more carefull after his being pardon'd, for his former to be abhorred Treasons and Villanyes by him committed under pretence of Astrology,) he hath committed an error of no lesse then forty six in time; and yet most impudently pretends to raise Judgments upon so deformed and false a foundation; and thence threatens the Grave Bishops and Churchmen; although Art it self speaks Eminently for them, as *Jupiter* in *Libra* upon the Cuspe of the 10th. in Reception of the Benigne Planet *Venus*, so likely and most aptly signifies.

Againe, in his figure of the Solar Eclipse

The Preface.

he is miftaken full 27. of time, and how much that will differ in Longitude let the Learned Artift judg. Yet, this fellow be his figures true or falfe, takes upon him to doom Kingdoms and families ruine; thefe errors committed under pretence of Art, befides particular and perfonall injuries by him committed againft, and reflected upon my perfon, I appeal to any unbyafed perfon, whether I have not juft caufe to unmaske this Impofter.

Mr. *Lilly*'s his Abilities are borrowed from Mr. *Nicholas Fisk*, *Culpeper* and others, who compofed his Books for him, both prefent and to come, and being not congenerous with the matter and the various annexes of it; I will never therefore anfwer him by word or writing, becaufe he is *Sterquilinii filius*, a fon of the Dunghill, and not able to fill the ftomack of the Learned Reader.

Ἅγι<Θ> ὁ Θεὸς, ἅγι<Θ> ἰχυρ<Θ>, ἅγι<Θ> ὁ ἀθάνατος ἐλέησον ἡμᾶς.

M. C. aA. ☐ ☉ & ♄. per *directionum*.

The

The Preface.

The Learned know he is an Impoſtor and no Schuller, the Aſtrologers know he is no Artiſt, and all other people know he is *a lying Sycophaticall Knave*, that hath gained out of ſimple people about 5col. *per annum* which he now enjoyes; but I ſhall not tread upon a worme, it is enough that he lyes at my feet, Here you ſee how *Botchers* would turn *Aſtrologers*, *Porters* practice the *Law*; *Coblers* Preach, and *Stocking-weavers*, *Hatband-makers*, and *Smiths*, &c. pretend to be *Doctors of Phiſick*: But I wiſh all ingenious men, not to confine their intelects to the narrow and cloudy Horizon of theſe mens dull braines, for they are as ſhort of theſe ſciences, as *Merlinus Anglicus*, and *Mother Shipton* are of *Stegnography*, and the *Mathematicks*; and are no more in my Harmony of Heaven and Earth, *then Lucians Luchonopters* or *Hoppogypians. Procul hinc procul ite prophani*, let the aſſe paſſe.

Now

The Preface.

Now will follow the Fæminine hearted fellows or scribling schoolmen brand me with their *Contra Principa*, and come with their Tophet, and a *Traditur Satane*, I know I shall be hated of most for my paines, because the *Moon* comes to the *Opposition* of *Mars*, the worser sort of Lawyers they will hate me and endeavour to bring false witnesses against me: because I have in my *Idea of the Law*, corrected his Errors, and prescribed good president of *Government* and *Law*, because here the ascendent comes to the opposition of Jupiter.; some Presbyters they will be angry also without cause, & will endeavour to imprison me, because I understand the policy of a Pulpit; the Phisitian he rages, because, the poor people are taught by me to cure themselves, here the Sun comes to the body of the *Moon*, and now I shall be scandalized and scoffed at like *Pythagorus* in *Lucian*, *Quis emit Heydonum*; *quis super Hominem esse vult*,

The Preface.

vult, quis scire universi Harmoniam, *& revivisere denuô*, thefe years are not troublefome only to me, but to all *Europe* and *London* will be *&c.* But becaufe an affirmative of this nature cannot fall to the ground with a Chriftian, I will come to my Oath; I do therefore proteft, before my glorious God, I have written it for the good health and help of all that ftand in need, hoping this with my other Books will be ferviceable, to all men, nor am I malicious, but zealous and affectionate to the truth of my creator, let fome Lawyer, Divines, *&c.* take heed then, leaft whiles they contemn Mifteries, they violate the Majefty of God in his creatures, and trample the blood of the covenant under foot: for I value not the envie of any man, becaufe I would reduce all to a harmony, and could wifh there were more love amongft Artifts, Now if any Divine, Philofopher, Aftronomer, Aftrologer, Geomancer, Chymift

The Preface.

:nift or Phyſitian, will write in oppoſition to my poſitions, I ſhall expect from him theſe following performances firſt, a poſitive expoſition of all the paſſages in my method of books and particularly in this, without any injury to the ſenſe of their Author: For if they interpret them otherwiſe then they ought, they but create error of their own, and then overthrow them; yet the ſtile I confeſſe is therefore the worſe, becauſe whileſt I was writing it, (which is fourteen years ſince and til now ſlept ſylently) I conſulted more with reaſon then with Rhetorick: But for my Doctrine it is not ſlightly proved.

Again ſecondly, I have borrowed no mans Authority, but ſuch as is eminent, and quotations I have left out purpoſely, becauſe I am not controverſial, it had been all one labour, to have given you both the Author and place, but it would have troubled the Text, or ſpotted the Margen,, which I wiſh may be free for the

Comments

The Preface.

Comments of him that reads, besides I do not professe my self a scholler, and for a Gentleman I hold it a little predanticall; now I professe the *Law* and practice it, according to my *Idea of the Law and Government*, and this method is also mine and hath relation to my *RosieCrucian Infallible Axiomata, The Temple of Wisdome* and *The Way to Blisse* which is made publick imperfect, but shall shortly be compleated, with a most excellent and mesterious experience, where I have lately seen, and with this *The Fundamentall Elements of Morrall Phylosophy, Policy, Government and the Lawes*; Thus you see I fear not the Airy Dart of any Cloudy brow, but desire peacably to do good to all men, let who will oppose us: Again, the Humerists, to prove their familiarity and knowledg in these sciences, must give the Reader a punctuall discovery of the secrets in them; if this be more then they can doe; it is argument enough they know not what they oppose: and if they do

The Preface.

do know; how can they Judge? or if they Judge where is their evidence to condemne? Let them not mangle and difcompofe my Books with a fcatter of obfervations, but proceed Methodically to the cenfure of each, expounding what is obfcure and difcovering the very practife, that the reader may finde my pofitions to be falf not only in their Theory; but if he will affay it, by his own particular experience.

Now I intreat all ingenious and well difpofed Gentlemen, that they would not flight my indeavours, becaufe of my years which are yet but few, It is the cuftome of moft men to meafure knowledg by the beard, and that they would not conclude any thing rafhly concerning the Method of thefe Books I have written, for they are not eafily apprehended, and yet I have fpoken as plainly as poffible, for the truths of thefe Arts and Sciences are almoft loft, and it is not my happinefs to know any man that understands

The Preface.

derstands them in their pure Easterne Glories.

To conclude at this time my present discourse, I wish it the common fortune of truth and honesty, to deserve well and hear ill, as for applause, I fish not so much in the Air as to catch it, it is a kinde of popularity, a froth and verball crack in the Pamphlet womens laps in *London* streets, and in Pedlers packs to be seen every day in Almanacks, which makes me scorne it, for I defie the noise of the rout, because they observe not the truth, but the successe of it, I do therefore commit this peice to the world, with the protection of a Gentleman more learned then my self, and the estimat of that soul that understands it, for the rest as I cannot force, so I will not beg their approbation, I would not be great by Imposts nor rich by briefs, they may be what they will, and I shall be what I am willing to do good to the honest Artists; and willing to do Justice

The Preface.

to those that are wronged in vexatious Lawsuits, and willing to cure the diseased.

From my House next door to the Red Lyon *on the East side* Spittle-Fields *near* Bishopsgate, London, September ☌ *the* 10th. 9h. 45. P. M. 1662.

John Heydon.

To

To the Readers.

Gentlemen,

I Thought good to let you know, that Mr. John Heydon hath written a body of Morral Phylosophy, Policy, Government, Laws, Rosie Crucian rules, Natural Phylosophy and Medicines, *in such order and upon such Principles, as are used by men, conversant in Demonstration:* These he hath distinguished into ten Books, viz. 1. The Holy Guide in *four Books, the last* of Projection. 2. The Wisemans Crown. 3 The new method of Rosie Crucian Phyick. 4. The Caballa or Art, by which they say *Moses* shewed so many miraculous signes in *Ægypt*, and *Joshua* made the Sun and Moon stand still. 5. The Rosie Crucian Infallible Axiomata. 6. The Fundamental

The Preface.

damental Elements of Morral Phyloſophy, Policy, Government and Laws. 7. The Idea of the Law. 8. The Idea of Government. 9. The Idea of Tyranny; And 10. The Temple of Wiſdome: *Each of the conſequents begining at the end of the Antecedent, and inſiſting there upon, as the latter Books of* Eucclid *upon the former; ſome of theſe he hath already publiſhed in* Itally: *The firſt* 3d, 6th. 5th. 7th. *and* 10. *with this ſo much deſired by;* The learned were preſerved by the good hand of God from the Tyrants of the times, *who perſecuted his perſon, and forced his Father and him to pay two thouſand pound, being taken in Arms for the King*, and alwayes he uſed to pray for the King and Biſhops.

Theſe Books are printed and publiquely preſented to the world, and if they receive Juſtice, *there is hopes we may obtain more:* He whoſe care *it is and* labour *to ſatisfie,* teach *and* direct *the* judgment, *and* Reaſon *of* Mankinde, *will condeſcend ſo farre (we hope) to content the deſire of*

The Preface.

of those learned men, whom these shall either have found, or made, which cannot be, untill they shall Analytically have followed the grand Phænomena of Nature, through States and Kingdomes in their Passions, into the Elemental principles of Natural and Corporeal Motions: This Book relates to all the rest, and we are much indebted to him for these most admirable Treatises so Harmoniously composed.

R. H.

To his approved Friend,

Mr. *JOHN HEYDON*, on his many learned and painful labours already published, and on this particular Excellent Piece of Phylosophy, entituled, *The Harmony of the World.*

M*Oſt* ſtudious friend! *thy conſtant* Bookiſh cares,
Will on thy head *full ſoon pull* ſilver hairs:
They'l keep thee waking, while the world's at reſt,
And bring thy ſmoother face *unto the teſt*
Of Age and Wrinkles; *make thy* Spring-like brow,
To feel the force of Key*&* crooked Plough
Before thy time, unleſs thy kinder Fate,
Such cruel deſtiny *anticipate-*
Is't Common Good *that makes thee labour thus?*
Or Gain *compels thee to be kind to us?*
If't be the Laſt, *thou ſhooteſt wide the mark;*
Unleſs by Gain *we underſtand ſome ſpark,*
Or flame of Natures Myſt'ries) *if the* Firſt,
Thy profit *loudly vouches that the worſt:*

d 4   For

For what is he would macerate his brains,
To get *sic vos non vobis* for his pains?
Then both wayes we conclude, thy Noble Brain,
Contemns and scorns all rusty common gain.
Thy open brest unto all Europe shows
Learning, and all things Gratis, as it knows.
Go on then Friend; so shall all Schoolmens
　praise,
On thy deserving head let fall the Bayes;
And deck thy Brows with Lawrel Wreaths:
　(for why)
Thy Merits claim them for this Harmony:
Thy publick Spirit mixt with equal parts,
Doth seal each man a debtor to thy Arts:
Thou shin'st so bright upon all; Thus the Sun
Illum'es the whole world, receives Light
　from none.

　　　　　　John Gadbury, Φιλομαθματικȣ.

Upon the Harmony of the
*World, now published by my much ho-
noured and ingenious Friend,*
Mr. JOHN HEYDON.

Harmonicos cantabo modos, humerosq; canoros.

A Way with discord; Harmony appears,
And is resplendant in our *British spheres*:
Thrice seven years have the Clouds of Ignorance
Obscured Learning : Now a glorious glance
Shoots forth, and all the croaking Frogs expells,
Which troubled have our Hippocrenian Wells.
Is th' World in Harmony? our English world?
No ! late it was into confusion hurl'd,
Till our true-born *Apollo Python* slew,
And purg'd the ayr of its infectious dew,
Which nipt the budding of the forward Spring,
And clipt the soaring of true Learnings Wing.

Is

Is *France* with *Spain*, or *Spain* with *France* at
   War?
Cannot they walk, or talk, but must they
   jar?
Can none agree them? Discord then pack
   hence;
How sweet is Harmony in every sence?
The Fire and Water, Ayr and Earth agree
In compound mixtures, make sweet Harmo-
   ny:
There is a Chain of Concord down de-
   scends,
From Heaven to Earth, and from the Earth
   ascends
To heaven: To this I willingly submit,
Our Author doth the *Diapason* hit:
For he that is at concord with himself,
Needs not fear shipwrack upon Discords
   shelf.

Octob. 8. 1661.

              Sic cecinit, *John Booker* Φιλαρμονικὸς.

To his ingenious Friend,

Mr. *JOHN HEYDON*, upon his most Elegant discourse, entituled, *The Harmony of the World*.

NO Heteroclites, *nor* Anomalae's,
Are found in Natures Language , *all her Laws*
Unlike to ours, admit of no repeal,
No alterations by a Commonweal :
No Heterogenious members do foment
Divisions there, without a Parliament :
As Soveraign she maintains her Regency,
And thus subdues the World to Harmony :
Spirits stand ready to administer.
The meanest Province *is assign'd by her :*
No jarring principles entered the frame,
Which she at first compos'd, the very name
Of a Litigious Eris *was unknown,*
And all melodiously conspir'd in one :
By favour of a Figure, *now they prove,*
That Planets do in an Elipsis *move*:
But there's no Motions *are Eccentrical*
In proper speech, *because they're Natural.*

A ij

All Musick is not (as it now appears)
Monopolized by the highest spheres;
Gammut as well as Ela bears its part,
Natures Vestigia shew themselves in Art,
How the Cœlestial Emissaries act
Their parts with mortals, and how they transact
Their own affairs; how man may lay the Scene
Above the stars, and what doth intervene
'Twixt matter and unbodied souls, that sense
May have free trade with an intelligence,
How man may traffique with the world unknown,
And have good company when he's alone;
How Hysteron and Proteron do twine
About each other, how extremes combine;
How subtil Aporrhea's propagate
Gross matter, and corruptions generate;
How nothing is exuberant nor mist,
Here's to be shewn by Natures Anylist.

Tho. Fyge, Gent.

To the most Excellent

Phylosopher and Lawyer M. John Heydon, *upon the so much desired* Harmony of the World.

A Publick good must quell your private fear,
The profit of a Writers *industry*,
Should be imparted to a general ear,
For good is better'd by community:
Nor may detraction, or the injury
Of some mens censures dash what he doth write,
If but what only pleaseth all mens sight,
No work would come to light, no work should come to light.
Through all the world y' 'ave gather'd the several flowers
Of other books into your *Harmony*;
Distill'd to Spirit by you, they're wholly yours,
So honey suckt from the variety
Of flowers, is yet the honey of the Bee:
And though in these last daies Miracles are fled,
Yet this shall of your *Harmony* be read,
It brings back time that's past, and gives life to the Dead.

J.B. D.D. Q.C. *Oxon.*

The Harmony of the WORLD.

Chap. I.

Of God and his power in infusing of vertues and Idea's into things gradually, and how the Soule from God descends into the Body; that the nature of God is as intelligible as the nature of any being whatsoever; the true notion of his ubiquity, and how inteligible it is, of the Union of Divine Essence; of the Notion of a Spirit, of the Office and Duty of Spirits, from Superiours to Inferiours.

GOD is a Spirit Eternal, Infinite in Essence and Goodnesse, Omniscient, Omnipotent, and of himself necessarily existent; He is a Globe of Light, whose Centre is every where, and Circumference no where; he inhabits the top of all the *Heavens*, and beholds

beholds all things that he hath Created: There are some Properties, Powers, and Operations imediately appertaining to him, of which no Reason can be given nor ought to be demanded; nor the way or manner of the Cohæsion of the Attribute with the subject can by any means be fancied or imagined.

In the second Region stand *ten spirits*, which are substances *penetrable* and *indiscerpible*, they are principal names of *God*, or as it were his members, that have *Divine powers* by *Instruments*, *Vestments*, or *Exemplars* of the *Archetype*; these transfer influence on all things Created; through the high things, even to the lowest, yet by a certain order; for first and imediately, they have influence on the nine Orders of *Angels*, and quire of blessed souls, and by them into the *Celestial Sphears*, *Planets* and *Men*.

The first of these Lights is called *Eheie*, and he is attributed to God the Father and Rules *Cether*, who carries the most simple Essence of the Divinity to *Hajoth Hakados*, who beareth the Creatures of Holinesse, to the *Angel Metattron*, and he delivers them to *Reschith*, *Hagalalim*, the Spirit that guides the *primum mobi'e*, that bestows the gift of being to all things, his Office in *Heaven* is to bring
othe

other *Angels* and *Genii* to the face of the King, and by him the *Prince* spake to *Moses*.

The second light is called *Jod Tetragrammaton*, and he is attributed to the second Person, *Jesus Christ*, and at his command *Hochma* sends influence to *Ophanim*, who carries it to *Jophael* and to the *Angel Masloh*, that rules *the spheare of the Zodiack*, where he fabricateth so many figures as he hath *Idea's* in himself, and distinguisheth the *Chaos* of the Creatures into three portions; of the first is made the spiritual world, of the second the visible heavens and their lights; but the third and worst part, was appointed for this sublunary building; out of this courſe and remaining portion was extracted the Elemental Quintessence or first matter of all things, and of this the foure Elements, and all those Creatures that inhabite them, by a particular spirit called *Raziel*, who was the ruler of *Adam*.

The third Spirit is called *Elohim Jehovah*, and is attributed to the *Holy Ghost*, he commands *Binah*, who sends his influence to *Aralim*, and then to *Zaphkiel*, then to *Sabatthi* the *Angel* that rules the ſphear of *Saturn*; this is the *principium generationis*, the beginning of the wayes of God, or the manifestation of the Father and Son's light, in the ſuperpernatural generation, from these come all living Souls, descending from the third light to the fourth day, thence to the fifth, whence they passe out & enter the night of the body, giving form to unsetled matter.

 Now you must understand that there are three supreme Lights, which rule and give power to these; and from this third light do the Souls descend to Flesh: but their pre-existency is in the *Ætherial Region*; indeed the *Æther* is a most thin liquid substance, above the Stars in the Circumference of the Divine Light, which receives the influent heat of God, and conveys it to the visible Heaven, and all the inferiour Creatures: It is a pure Essence, a thing not tainted with any material contagion, it is placed next to the Divine fire; it is the first Receptacle of the influences, and derivations of the supernatural world, which sufficiently confirms our *Etymologie*: In the beginning it was generated by reflection of the first unity upon the Cœlestial Cube, for the bright Emanations of God did flow like a stream into the passive πηγή, you shall understand that the *Ether* is not one but manifold, by this I mean not a variety of substances, but a chain of Complections, there are other Moistures and those too *Etheriall*, they are Females a

The Harmony of the World.

so of the *Masculine Divine Fire*, and these are the Fountains of the *Chaldean Astrologers*, which the *Oracle* Styles, *summitates fontanus*, the invisible upper springs of Nature. Of all substances that come to our hands, this *Ether* is the first that brings us News of another world, as tells us we live in a Corrupt one, it is the Urine of *Saturn*, and with it do I water my *Plants* of the *Sun* and *plants* of the *Moon*, which by it are Animated with a vegitable blessed Divine Fire, if you can obtain the knowledge of it, for it is to be found every where, *you will have a wonderfull Medicine that will alter, change and amend the state of the body, it prolongs life, preserveth Health, it maketh old men, young, wise and vertuous, &c.*

I have seen it tincture, *Cloth, Silkes, Lead, Iron, Tin, Copper, Gold, Silver*, with a thousand Miraculous *Colours*, being prepared by Art, it will look like *Rosialls* and *Rubies*, sometimes *violet Blew*, sometimes *White* as *Lillies*, and a small *Matter* will turn it more *Green* then *Grasse*, but with a *smaragdine Transparancy*, and again it will look like *Burnisht Gold* and *Silver*; it may be reduced to such a temper & so Qualified by Art, it will be fit to give any colour whatsoever, and now I passe into another Region.

The fourth Light is *Ell*, who Rules *Hesed* and

and sends Influence to *Hasmallim*, who carries Grace, Goodnesses, Mercy, Piety & Magnificence to the *Angel Zadkiel*, which *Ledek* passeth through the Sphere of *Jupiter*, fashioning the Images of bodies, bestowing clemency, and purifying Justice on all, but let us look back again, you must understand that the *third Person* is the last of the three, and sits equall in Power with *the Father and Son*; we read that *God* breathed into *Adam* the breath of life, and he became a living soul, and to *breath* is the property of the *holy Ghost* in order to operation, for he applyes first to the Creature, and therefore works first, (*i. e.*) The *Holy Ghost* could not breath a soul into *Adam*, but he must either receive it, or have it of himself: Now the truth is, he receives it, and what he receives, that he breaths into Nature, Hence this most holy spirit is stiled by the *Rosie Crutians*, *fluvius egrediens è paradiso*, because he breaths as a River streams: He is called also *Mater Filiorum*, because by his breathing he is as it were delivered of those souls which have been conceived *Ideally* in the second Person. Now that the *Holy Ghost* receives all things from the second Person, is confirmed by *Christ* himself, *Joh.* 16. 13. *When the spirit of truth is come, he will guide you into all truth, for he shall not speak of himself,*

but

but whatsoever he shall hear, that shall he speak; and he will shew you things to come; He shall glorifie me, for he shall receive of mine, and shall shew it unto you: All things that the Father hath are mine, Therefore said I, that he shall take of mine. Here we plainly see, there is a Certain subsequent order or Method in the operations of the blessed Trinity, For Christ tells us, that he receives from his *Father*, and the *Holy Ghost* receives from him: Again that all things are Conceived Ideally (or as we Commonly expresse it) created by the second Person, is confirmed by the word of *God*, *The world was made for him* (saith the Scripture) *and the world knew him Not, He came unto his own and his own received him Not*: Let this suffice to warrant our way, let us go forward.

The *Fifth* Light is named *Elohim Gibor*, who giveth the influence to *Geburah*, who carries it by the *Seraphim* to *Camael* the Angel of *Medim* through the Sphere of *Mars*; to these belong Fortitude, War, Affliction, the sword, and left hand of God.

The sixth Light is called *Eloha*, he hath his influence through *Malachim*, *Raphel*, *Schemes*, into the *Sphere* of the *Sun*, giving brightness and life to it, and from thence produceth mettalls.

The seventh light is called *Adonay Sabaoth*, he

he passeth his influence by *Nezah Elohim*, *Haniel* by the Angel *Noga* into the Sphere of *Venus*; it gives zeal and love of Righteousnes, and produceth vegetables.

The eighth Spirit is called *Elohim Sabaoth* and he Rules *Hod*, and hath his Influence by *Ben Elohim* to the angel *Michael*, Lord of *Cochab*, Through the Sphere of *Mercury*. Now these Angells are the *Souls* of the *Planets* and give life, light, & motion to them, to transfer it unto the Earth; after this order doth he give Elegancy and Consonancy of speech, and produceth Living Creatures.

The ninth *Light* is named *Sadai*, and he Rules *Jesod*, and hath his Influence by *Cherubim* to *Gabriel*, and through *Levanah* the Sphere of the *Moon*, causing the increase and decrease of all things, and taketh care of the *Genii* & *keepers of men*, and distributeth them.

The tenth *Light* is named *Adonoy Melech*, and he Governs *Malchuth*, and hath his Influence by *Issim* to the soule of *Messiah*, into *Helom Jesodoth* the sphere of the *Elements*, and giveth knowledge and the wonderfull understanding of things And thus God works by the *Idea*'s of his own Mind, and the *Idea*'s dispence their Seals, and communicate them daily to the Matter; now the *Anima mundi* hath in the fixed stars her particular forms, or seminall conceptions answerable to the *I-*

dea's of the Divine minde: and here doth she receive those spirituall powers and Influences, which originally proceed from *God*; from this place they are conveyed to the *Planets*, especially to the *Sun* and *Moon*, these two great lights impart them to the *Aire*, and from the *Aire* they passe down to the belly or Matrix of the Earth, in prolifix spirited winds and water; thus have I declared to you the descent of the secret power of Nature from God even to this Earth.

An Emanative cause is the Notion of a thing possible, an Emanative Effect is Coexistent with the very substance of that which is said to be the cause thereof; No Emanative Effect, that exceeds not the vertues and powers of a cause can be said to be impossible to be produced by it, and there may be a substance of that high virtue and excellency, that it may produce another substance by *Emanative* causality, provided that the substance produced be in due graduall proportions inferiour to that which causes it; and thus have I demonstrated how the Center or first point of the primary substance of a spirit may be indiscerpible, and how the secondary substance of a spirit may be indiscerpible, and how every thing receives life and vertue: from the highest *Angell* even to the Lowest *seminall Form*. Chap.

Chap. II.

Of the Nature of God and Spirits, how they are intelligible, a plain and compendious demonstration that Matter consists of parts indiscerpible. An Answer to William Lilly touching his simple conceits and flattering Predictions and Observations. An Apology for the vehicles of Demons and souls separate; of the state of the other life, that it is n t one universal soule that hears, sees and reasons in every man, demonstrated from the Acts of memory, of the spirits of Nature.

WE have in the last Chapter cleered the passage of Spirits from *Heaven* to *Earth*, and here we will make known their Nature; the Schoolmen hold that even the *purest Angels* have *Corporeal vehicles* But it will be hard for them to alledge any Antient Authority for their opinion: For *Aristotle* their Great Oracle is utterly silent in this Matter, as not believing the existence of *Demons* in the world (as Mr. *John Owen* and *Will. Lilly* his sworne disciple have to their great contentment taken notice off.) And therefore being left to their own dry subtilties, flatteries and deceits, they made all intellectuall beings that are not grossely *terrestriall*, as man is, purely *Immaterial*, wherby they make

a

The Harmony of the World.

a very hidious chasme or gaping breath in the order of things, such as no Moderate Judgment will ever allow of, & have become very obnoxious to be foyled by Atheisticall wits, who are forward and skilfull enough to draw forth the absurd consequences that ly hid in falf suppositions, as *Merlinus* the jugler dos in this, for he dos not foolishly collect from the supposed pure imateriallity of Demons, that they have no knowledg of particular things upon Earth, such pure incorporeal Essences being uncapable of impression from Corporeall Objects, and therefore have not the species of any particular thing that is Corporeal in their mind; whence he hath learnt this Inference, that all *Apparitions, Prophecies, Predictions, Prodigies,* and whatsoever miraculous is recorded in antient History, is not to be Attributed to these, but to the influence of the *Stars,* and so concludes that there are no such things as *Demons* in the universe.

By which kinde of reasoning also, it is easy for the *Pfychopannychites* to support their opinion of the sleep of the soul, for the soule being utterly rescinded from all that is Corporeall, and having no vitall Union there with at all, they will be very prone to infer, ᵹ it is impossible she should know any thing, *ad extra*, if she can so much as dream: For even that power also may seem incompetible to her in such a state, she having such an Essentiall aptitude for vitall Union, with matter of so great Consequence; it is sometimes to desert the Opinion of the Schools, when something more rational and more safe and usefull offers it self unto us.

The most common exception I foresee that will be against me, is, that I have taken upon me to describe the Nature and descent of *Angels* and *Genii* of the other world so punctually and particularly, as if I had been lately amongst them: For over exquisitenesse may seem to smell of *Art* and *Fraud*; and as there is a diffidency many times in us when we hear something that is extream suitable to our desire, being then most ready to think it too good to be true: So also in Notions that seem over accurately fitted to our intellectual Faculties, and agree the most natural therewith; we are prone many times to suspect them to be too easie to be true; especially in things that seemed at first to us very obscure and intricate; for which cause also it is very likely that the Notion of a particular spirit, which I have so accurately described in my first Book of *Geomancy* and *Telesmes*, entitled, *The Temple of Wisdome*,

may

may seem the lesse credible to some, because it is now made so clearly intelligible, they thinking it utterly improbable that these things, that have been held alwayes such inextricable perplexities, should be thus of a sudden made manifest and Familiar to any that hath but a Competency of patience and Reason to peruse the Theory.

They that deny my Doctrine and graduall descent of *Spirits* orderly going before, say that there is but one *soule* in the *World*, whose perceptive power is every where. Now they must assert, that what one part thereof perceives, all the rest perceives, or else that perceptions in *Demons*, *Men* and *Brutes* are confined to that part of this *soule* that is in them, while they perceive this or that. If the former, they are confutable by sence and experience. For though all animalls lie steeped, as it were, in that subtle Matter which runs through all things, and is the immediate instrument of sense and perception; yet we are not Conscious of one anothers thoughts, nor feel one anothers pains and pleasures of Brutes, when they are in them at the highest, nor yet do the *Demons* feell one anothers *affections*, or necessarily assent to one anothers *opinions*, though their vehicles be exceeding pervious,

else

else they would be all *Pythagorians* as well as those I speak of in *The Rosie Crurian, Infallible Axiomata.* Wherefore we may generally conclude, that if there were such an *Universal Soule*, yet the particular perceptions thereof, are restrained to this or that part in which they are made, which is contrary to the unity of a soul, as I shall tell you in its due place.

But let us grant the thing (for indeed we have demonstrated it to be so, if there be such an universal soul and none but it) then the grand absurdity comes in, which I was intimating before, *viz* that part of the soul of the world that never perceived a thing, shall notwithstanding remember it, that is to say, that it shall perceive, it hath perceived, that which it never perceived.

And yet one at *Tardebick* in *Warwick-shire* may remember, a man he had seen about twenty years before at *Venice* in *Italy*, being come into these parts a stranger; nay, which is more to the purpose: Supposing the *earth move*, what I write now, the *Earth being in the latter degree of* Pisces, I shall remember that I have written when she is in the *latter degree of* Virgo, though that part of the soule of the world that possesses my Body then will be twice as distant from what does guide
my

my hand to write now, As the *Earth* is from the *Sun*: wherefore it is plain, that such an universe soule will not solve all *Phænomena*, but there must be a particular soul in every man. And yet I dare say, this wilde opinion is more tenable than theirs, that make nothing but meer matter in the world: but I thought it worth the while, with all diligence to Confute them both; the better of them being but a more refined kinde of *Ætheisme*, tending to the subversion of the Fundamentals of *Religion* and *Piety* amongst men.

As for the Spirit of Nature, and soule of the world, I shall speak of them in their places, and of the *Harmony of the World*, and of *Man, and his Spirit*, the greatest exceptions are, that I have introduced an obscure principle for Ignorance and Sloth to take Sanctuary in. But to proceed by degrees to our main designe, and to lay our Foundation low and sure; we will in the first place expose to view the genuine Notion of a Spirit, in the general exception thereof, and afterwards of several kinds of Spirits, that it may appear to all, how unjust this cavill is against incorporeall substances, as if they were meer impossibilities and Contradictions in consistencies; I will define a spirit in generall thus,

thus, *A substance penetrable and indiscerpible*, The fitnesse of which definition will be the better understood, if we divide substance in general, into these first kinds, viz. *Body* and *spirit*, and then define *body* to be a *substance impenetrable & discerpible*, whence the contrary kind to this is fitly defined *a substance penetrable* and indiscerpible:

Now I appeal to any man that can set aside prejudice; and has the free use of his faculties, whether every terme in the Definition of a spirit be not as intelligible and Congruous to Reason, as in that of a body, for the precise Notion of a substance is the same in both, in which, I conceive, is comprised *extention* & *activity*, either Connate or communicated, for matter it self once moved can move other matter, and it is as easy to understand what *penetrable* is, as *impenetrable*, and what *indiscerpible* as *discerpible*; and *penetrability* and *indiscerpibility* being as immediate to *spirit*, as *impenetrability* and *discerpibility* of *body*, there is as much reason to be given for the Attributes of the one as of the other, as you may remember from the first Chapter: And substance in its precise Notion including no More of *impenetrability* then *indiscerpibility*, we may as well wonder how one kinde of substance can so firmely and

and irresistably keep out another substance (as matter for example does the parts of matter) as that the parts of another substance hold so fast together, that they are by no means discerpible, as we have already intimated.

And therefore this holding out in one, being as difficult a businesse to conceive, as the holding together of the other, this can be no prejudice to the Notion of a Spirit; For there may be very fast union where we cannot at all imagine the Cause thereof, as in such bodies which are exceeding hard, where no man can fancy what holds the parts together so strongly; and there being no greater difficulty here, than that a man cannot imagine what holds the parts of a Spirit together, it will follow, *That, what is plainly and manifestly concluded, ought to be held undeniable, when no difficulties are alledged against it, but such as are acknowledged to be found in other conclusions, held by all men undeniably true*: As for example, Suppose one should conclude, *that there may be infinite matter*, or *That there is infinite space*, by very rational Arguments; and that it were objected onely, that then the tenth part of the Matter would be infinite; it being most certain, that there is infinite *duration* of something or other in the world; and that the tenth part of this duration is infinite: It is no enervating at all of the former Conclusion; it being incumbred with no greater incongruity, than is acknowledged to consist with an undeniable Truth; now the notion of a *Spirit* is not to be excepted against, as an incongruous Notion, but is to be admitted for the Notion of a thing that may really exist.

It may be doubted, whether there may not be *Essences* of a *middle Condition* betwixt these *Corporeal* and *Incorporeal Lights* and *Substances* we have described, and that of two sorts; that one *impenetrable* and *discerpible*, the other *penetrable* and *indiscerpible*; but concerning the first, if *impenetrability* be understood in reference to Matter, it is plain there can be no such Essence in the world. And if in reference to its own parts, though it may then look like a possible *Idea* in it self; yet there is no footstep of its existence thereof in Nature, the *souls* of *Men* and *Demons* implying contraction and dilatation in them; As for the latter, it has no priviledge for any thing more than matter it self hath, or some mode of matter. For it being discerpible, it is plain its union is by juxtaposition of parts, and the more penetrable, the lesse likely

ikely to conveigh sense and motion to any
listance; besides, the ridiculous sequel of
his supposition, that will fill the Universe
with an infinite number of *Shreds* and *Rags*
of *Souls* and *Spirits*, never to be reduced a-
ain to any use or order.

And lastly, the proper notion of a sub-
tance incorporeal, fully counter distinct to
corporeal substance, necessarily including
n it so stronge and indissolvable Union of
arts, that it is utterly indiscerpible, when
s yet for all that in this general Notion
hereof, neither sense nor cogitation is im-
lyed; it is most rational to conceive that
iat substance wherein they are, must assu-
:dly be incorporeal in the strictest significa-
.on: The Nature of Cogitation and Com-
1union of Sense arguing a more perfect de-
ree of Union than is in meer indiscerpibili-
y of parts. But all this scrupulosity might
ave been saved; for I confidently promise
1y self, that there are none so perversely
iven to tergiversations and subterfuges;
ut that they will acknowledge, where ever
can prove that there is a Substance distinct
om Body or Matter, that it is in the most
ill and proper sense Incorporeal.

Chap. III.

That the Idea's of several kindes of Immaterial beings: have no inconsistency, nor incongruity in them, of the Idea of God and his Power, of all Finite and Created Spirits: how they are defined of Indiscerpibility : *A symbolical representation thereof; an Objection answered against that representation; an Application of principles of the Union of the secondary substance, considered transversly, that the* Idea *of a Spirit hath less difficulty than that of Matter An Answer to an Objection from the Rational faculty: Answers to the* Hypothesis *of Fancy, of the self motion of a Spirit, of self Penetration, of self Contraction and Dilatation, the Power of Penetrating of Matter, The power of moving and of altering the Matter.*

I Have shewn that the *Idea* of a Spirit in general is not at all incongruous nor impossible: And it is as congruous, consistent and intelligible in the sundry kinds thereof. As for example, that of God, of Angels, of *the souls of Men* and *Brutes,* and of the λόγοι σπερματικοί, or, *Seminal Forms* of things.

The *Idea* of *God*, though the knowledge thereof be much prejudiced by the Confoundednes and stupidity of either Superstitious

itious, *Anabaptists*, or profane *Atheists* that please themselves in their large Lords Word, concerning the *unconceivableneß* and utter *incomprehensibleneß* of the *Deity*; the one by way of a Devotional Exaltation of the transcendency of his Nature, the other to make the belief of his Existence rediculous, and craftily and perversely to intimate that there is no God at all, the very conception of him being made to appear nothing else but a bundle of inconsistencies and impossibilities: Neverthelesse, I shall not at all stick to affirm, that his *Idea* is as easie as any *Idea* else whatsoever, and that we may know as much of him as of any thing else in the world; for the very Essence or naked Substance of Nothing can possible be known thus: *The subject or naked Essence or substance of a thing, is utterly unconceivable to any of our Faculties.*

For Demonstration of this Truth, there needs nothing more than a silent appeal to a mans own mind, if he does not finde it so: and that he take away all *Aptitudes*, *Operations*, *Properties* and *Modifications* from a *subject*, that his Conception thereof vanishes into Nothing, but into the *Idea* of a meer indiversificated substance; so that one substance is not then distinguishable from another;

ther; but onely from *Accidents* or *Modes*, to which properly belongs no Substance: But for Attributes, they are as Conspicuous as the Attributes of any subject or substance, whatsoever; as I defined him in the first Chapter, *viz. God is a Spirit eternal, Infinite in Essence and Goodness, Omniscient, Omnipotent, and of himself necessarily Existent.* For *a Spirit* I have explained already, and by *Eternal*, I understand nothing here, but duration without end or beginning, by *Infiniteness of Essence*, that his Essence hath no bounds, no more than his Duration: by Infinite in Goodness, such a benign will in God, as is carried out to boundlesse and innumerable benefactions: by *Omnisciency* and Omnipotency, the ability of knowing or doing any thing that can be conceived without a plain contradiction; by *self-Existency* that he cannot faile to be. What terms of any Definition are more plain than these of this; or what subject can be more accurately defined than this is? For the naked subject or substance of any thing is no otherwise to be known then thus; and they that gape after any other speculative knowledge of *God* then what is from his Attributes and Operations, they may have their heads filled with *fiery fancies*, and their *mouths with burning words.*

words, and run mad with the boisterousnes of their own imagination, but they will never hit upon any sober truth.

Thus have I delivered a very explicite and intelligible *Idea* of the nature of God; which I might also more compendiously define, an Essence absolutely perfect, in which all the terms of the former Definition are comprehended, and more than I have named, or thought needfull to name, much lesse to insist upon; as his power of Creation and his Omnipresence or Ubiquity, which are necessarily included in the *Idea* of absolute perfection; The latter whereof some antient Philosophers endeavouring to set out, have defined *God to be a Globe of Light, a Circle whose Centre is every where, and Circumference no where*, by which description certainly nothing else can be meant, but that the Divine Essence is every where present with all those Adorable Attributes of Infinite

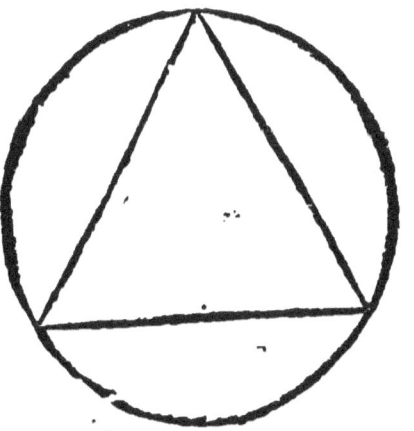

and absolutely perfect Goodnesse, Knowledge,

ledge and Power; according to the sense in which I have explained them, which Ubiquity or Omnipresence of *God*, is just as intelligible as the overspreading Matter in to all places.

But if there be any *Novice Astrologer* demand how the parts, as I may so call them, of the Divine Amplitude hold together, that of Matter being so discerpible; it might be sufficient to remind him, of what we have already spoken of the general *Idea* of a Spirit: But besides that, here may be also a peculiar, rational account given thereof; it implying a contradiction, that an *Essence* absolutely perfect, should be either limited in presence, or change place in part or whole; they being both notorious effects or simptoms of imperfection, which is inconsistent with the Nature of *God*; And no better nor more cogent reason can be given of any thing then that it implies a contradiction to be otherwise.

That power also of Creating things of Nothing, there is a very close connexion betwixt that and the *Idea* of *God*, or of a being absolutely perfect, for this being would not be what it is conceived to be; if it were destitute of the power of Creation, and therefore this Attribute hath no lesse coherence with

with the subject, than that it is a contradiction, it should not be in it, as was observed of the foregoing attribute of indiscerpibility in God; but to alleadge that a man cannot imagine how *God* should create something of nothing, or how the *Divine Essence* holds so closely and invincibly together, is to deny, That, *all our faculties have not a right of suffrage for determining of Truth, but onely common Idea's, external sense, and evident and undeniable deductions of Reason*; Hereby *common Ideas or Notions* I understand whatever is *Nomatically* true, (*i. e.*) true at first sight, to all *Heydonians* or men in their wits, upon a clear perception of the Terms, without any further discourse or reasoning from *external sense*; I conclude not memory, as it is a faithfull register thereof, and you cannot appeal to a faculty that hath no right to determine the case: We have now sufficiently spoken of the *Idea* of that Infinite and *uncreated spirit*, we usually call *God*: We will passe now on our way into another Region, to those *Spirits* that are *Created* and *Finite*, as the *spirits* of *Angels, Planets, Stars, Men* and *Brutes*; we will cast in the *seminal Forms* also or *Archei*, as the *Rosie Crucians* call them, though haply the world stands in no need of them. The properties of a *spirit*, as it is an *Idea* common to all these,

1

I have already enumerated in my *New Method of Rosie Crucian Physick*, self-motion, self-penetration, self-contraction, and dilatation, and indivisibility, by which I mean indiscerpibility: To which I added *penetrating, moving,* and *altering the Matter*, we may therefore define this kinde of *Spirit* we speak of, to be a *substance indiscerpible, that can move it self; that can penetrate, contract and dilate it self;* and can also *penetrate, move* and *alter the matter:* I shall now examine every term of this definition, from whence it shall appear, that it is as congruous & intelligible, as those Definitions that are made of such things as *men,* without any scruple, acknowledge to exist

I have given rational grounds, of the *indiscerpibility* of a *spirit,* to evince it not impossible, it being an imediate Attribute thereof, as impenetrability is of a body, and as conceivable or imaginable, that one substance of its own nature may invincibly hold its parts together; so that they cannot be disunited nor dissevered, as that another may keep out so stoutly and irresistibly another substance from entering into the same space or place with it self; for this ἀντιτυπία, or impenetrability is not at all contained in the precise Conception of a *Substance* as *Substance,*

The Harmony of the World.

ſtance, as I have already ſignified. But beſides that reaſon we may thus eaſily apprehend that it may be ſo; I ſhall a little gratifie imagination, and it may be reaſon too, in offering the manner how it is ſo, in this kinde of ſpirit I now ſpeak of. That ancient *Idea* of *Light* and *intentional ſpecies* is ſo from a plain impoſſibility, that has been heretofore generally, and is ſtill by Mr. *Tho. Heydon,* Dr. *Ward,* and other learned men looked upon as a truth; that is, That *Light* and *Colour* do ray in ſuch ſort, they are deſcribed in the *Roſie Crucian Phyloſophy*; Now it is obſervable in *light,* that it is moſt vigorous towards its fountain, and fainter by degrees. But we will reduce the matter to one lucid point, which according to the acknowledged principles of Opticks, will fill a diſtance of ſpace with its rayes of *light*: which rays may indeed be reverberated back towards their Centre, by interpoſing ſome Opake body, and ſo this orbe of *light* contracted; but according to the *Roſie Crucian Hypotheſis,* it was alwayes accounted impoſſible, that they ſhould be clipt off, or cut from this lucid point, and be kept a part by themſelves; Thoſe whom dry reaſon will not ſatisfie, ſhall have hard blows, or if they pleaſe, they may entertain their fancy with ſuch a Repreſentation as this,

this, which may a little ease the Anxious importunity of their mind, when it would too eagerly comprehend the manner how this spirit I speak of, may be said to be indiscerpible. For think of any ray of this *Globe* or *Orbe* of *Lights*, it does sufficiently set out to the imagination, how extention and indiscerpibility may consist together; see my Book, entitled, *The Temple of Wisdome*, as also, *The Wisemans Crown*, chap. 9.

But if any Object, that the lucid point of this Orbe, or the primary substance, as I call it, in my *RosieCrucian Infallible Axiomata*, cap. 3. is either divisible or absolutely indivisible, and if it be divisible, that as concerning the *inmost* of a *spirit*, this representation is not at all serviceable to set off the nature thereof; by shewing how the parts there may hold together so indiscerpibly, but if absolutely indivisible, that it seems to be nothing: To this I answer what Sr. *Chr. Heydon*, hath somewhere noted, *That what is infinitely great or infinitely small, the imagination of a man is at a loss to conceive it.* Which certainly is the ground of the perplexedness of that probleme concerning Matter, whether it consists of points, or onely of Particles divisible *in infinitum*, but to come more closely to the businesse; I say, that though we should acknowknowledge the inmost centre of life; or the very first point, as I may so call it, of the primary substance (for this primary substance is gradually to be purely indivisible, it does not at all follow, no not according to imagination it self, that it must be nothing. For let us imagine a perfect Plain, a Bowling-green bigger than *Salisbury Plain*, and on this Plain, the *Globe of Mercury*, we cannot conceive but this Globe touches the Plain, and that in what we ordinarily call a point, else the one would not be Globe, or the other not a Plain; Now it is impossible, that one body should touch another, and yet touch one another in nothing; Wherefore this inmost Centre of life is something, and something so full of essential vigour and virtue, that though gradually it diminish; yet can fill a certain *sphere* of space with its own presence and activity, as a spark of light illuminates the duskish Aire; wherefore there being no greater perplexity nor subtilty in the consideration of this Centre of life, or *inmost* of a *spirit*, then there is in the *Attomes* of Matter, we may now rightly conclude, that indiscerpibility hath nothing in the *Idea* thereof, but what may well consist with the possibility of the existence of the subject whereunto it belongs.

Let

Let us advance yet higher, and demonstrate the possibility of this *Idea* to the severest reason, out of these following Principles, *viz.* A *Globe* touches a Plain; admit for an Example one of Mr. *Jo Moxons* Globes, and one of Mr. *John Colins* his Plains: The Globe I say touches the Plain in something, though in the least, *that is conceivable to be reall*; *the least that is conceivable is so little, that it cannot be conceived to be discerpible into less*; *As little as this is, the repetition of it will amount to considerable magnitudes*: If this Globe be drawn upon a Plain, it constitutes a *line*, and a *Cylinder* drawn upon a Plain, or this same line described by the Globe multiplied into it self, constitutes a superficies, *&c.* This a man cannot deny, but the more he thinks of it, the more certainly true he will finde it.

Magnitudes cannot arise out of meer non-magnitudes; and if you multiply nothing ten thousand millions of times into nothing, the product will be still nothing: Besides, if that wherein the Globe touches a Plain, were more then indiscerpible, that is, purely Indivisible; it is manifest, that a *line* will consist of points Mathematically so called, that is, purely indivisible, which is the grandest absurdity that can be admitted in Philosophy, and the most contradictious thing imagi-

The Harmony of the World.

imaginable, the same thing by reason of its extream littleneſſe may be utterly indiſcerpible, though intellectually diviſible: For every quantity is intellectually diviſible; but ſomething indiſcerpible was afore demonſtrated to be quantity, and conſequently diviſible; otherwiſe Magnitude would conſiſt of Mathematical points: Thus have I found a poſſibility for *Idea of the Centre of a Spirit*; which is not a *Mathematical point*, but a ſubſtance in magnitude, ſo little, that it is Indiſcerpible; but in vertue ſo great, that it can ſend forth out of it ſelf, ſo large a ſphere of *ſecondary* ſubſtance, as I may ſo call it, that it is able to actuate grand proportions of matter; this whole ſphere of life and activity being in the mean time utterly indiſcerpible.

This I have ſaid, and ſhall now prove it by adding a few more principles of that evidence, I have written at the latter end of the firſt Chapter of this *Book*, and ſhall here ſo explain them, as the moſt rigorous reaſon ſhall not be able to deny; *An Emanative cauſe is the Idea or Notion of a thing poſſible*: Now by an Emanative cauſe is underſtood, as meerly by being, no other activity or cauſality interpoſed, produces an Effect; That this is poſſible, is manifeſt, it being demonſtrable,

strable, that there is *de facto*, some such cause in the world; because something must move it self; now if there be no Spirit, Matter must of necessity move it self, where you cannot imagine any Activity or Causality; but the bare Essence of the Matter from whence this motion comes: For if you would suppose some former Motion that might be the cause of this, then we might with as good reason suppose some former to be the cause of that, and so *in infinitum*

An Emanative Effect is coexistent with the very substance of that which is said to be the cause thereof. And this must needs be true, because that very substance which is said to be the cause, is the adequate and immediate cause, and wants nothing to be adjoyned to its bare Essence, for the production of the Effects: And therefore by the same reason the Effect is at any time; it must be at all times, or so long as that substance does exist. *No Emanative Effect, that exceeds not the vertues and powers of a Cause can be said to be impossible to be produced by it.*

There may be a substance of that high vertue and excellency, that it may produce another substance by Emanative Causallity; provided that substance produced be in due graduall proportions inferiour to that which causes it: Now there is
no

no contradiction nor impossibility of a Cause producing an effect lesse noble than it self; or thereby we are the better assured that it does not exceed the capacity of its own Powers: Nor is this any incongruity, that one Substance should cause something else, which we may in some sense call substance; though but *secondary* or *Emanatory*; acknowedging the *Primary Substance* to be the more adequate object of Divine Creation; but the secondary to be referrible also to the primary or *Central* substance, by way of causall relation: For suppose God created the Matter with an immediate power of moving it self; God indeed is the prime cause as well of the Motion as of the Matter; and yet neverthelesse the Matter is rightly said to move it self; Finally, this *secondary* or *Emanatory substance*, because it is a subject indued with certain powers and activities, and that it does not inhære as an accident in any other substance or matter, but could maintain its place, though all Matter or what other Substance soever were removed out of that space it is extended through, provided its *primary substance* be but safe.

From these four principles I have here again added from the first Chapter, we may have not an imaginary but rational apprehension

D.

hension of that part of Spirit, which we call the secondary substance thereof; whose extension arising by gradual Emanation from the first and primest Essence (as you read before in the first Chapter,) which we call *Centre* of the Spirit, which is no impossible supposition; we are led from hence to a necessary acknowledgment of perfect indiscerpibility of parts, though not intellectually Indivisibility, for that would imply a contradiction, that an Emanative effect should be disjoyned from its original.

Thus have I demonstrated the graduall descent of *Spirits*, and how a *spirit* considering the lineaments of it (as I may so call them) from the *Centre* to the *Circumference* is utterly indiscerpible: but now if any be so curious, as to ask how the parts thereof hold together in a line drawn crosse to these from the Centre; (for imagination, it may be, will suggest they lye all loose?) I Answer that the conjecture of imagination is here partly true and partly false, or is true or false, as she shall be interpreted; for if she be loose, actually disunited, it is false and rediculous: but if onely so discerpible, that one part may be disunited from another, that is not onely true but necessary; otherwise it could not contract one part and ex-
ten-

tend another, which is yet an Hypothesis necessary to be admitted: Wherefore this Objection is so far from weakening the possibility of this Notion, that it gives occasion more fully to declare the exact concinnity thereof; To be brief therefore, a Spirit from the Centre to the Circumference is utterly indiscerpible, but in lines crosse to this, it is closely cohærent, but not indiscerpibly; which cohæsion may consist in an imediate union of these parts, and transverse Penetration and Transcursion of a secondary substance, through this whole Sphere of life, which we call *Spirit*.

Nor need we wonder that so full an Orbe should swell out from so subtile and small a Point, as the Centre of this Spirit is supposed Εἰ γὰρ χỳ τῷ ὄγκῳ μικρὸν ἔξι, δυνάμει χỳ τιμιότητι πολὺ μᾶλλον ὑπερέχει πάντων, as *Plato* somewhere sayes of the minde of man: And besides it is but what is seen in some sort to the very eye in light, how large a sphere of Aire a little spark will illuminate; This is the pure *Idea* of a *created Spirit* in general, concerning which, if there be any cavill to be made, it can be no other then what is perfectly common to it and to Matter; that is, the unimaginablenesse of points, and smallest particles, and how what is discerpible

cannot

cannot at all hang together: but this is not hindering matter from actual Existence of a spirit, but the most lubricous Hypothesis that we go upon here, is not altogether so intricate as those difficulties in Matter. For if that be but granted, in which I finde no absurdity; that a particle of matter may be so little, that it is utterly uncapable of being made lesse; it is plain that one and the same thing, though intellectually divisible, may yet be really indiscerpible And indeed it is not onely possible, but it seems necessary that this should be true: For though we should acknowledge that matter were discerpible *in infinitum*, yet supposing a cause of infinite distinct perception, and as infinite power, (*and God is such*) this cause can reduce this capacity of infinite discerpibleness of Matter into act *viz.* actually, and at once discerp it, or disjoyn it into so many particles as it is discerpible into: From whence it will follow, that one of these particles reduced to this perfect parvitude, is then utterly indiscerpible; and yet intellectually divisible otherwise magnitude would consist of mee points, which would imply a contradiction We have therefore plainly demonstrated b reason, that Matter consists of parts indis cerpible; and therefore there being no othe
facult

faculty to give suffrage against it; for neither sense nor any common notion can contradict it; it remains, *Whatever is clear to any one of these three faculties, is to be held undoubtedly true, the other having nothing to evidence to the contrary*: Or else a man shall not be assured of any sensible object that he meets with, nor can give firm assents to such truths as these; It is impossible the same thing should be, and not be, at once; whatever is, is either Finite or Infinite, &c. and thus doe I prove my Conclusion true.

What some would object from Reason, that these perfect parvitudes being acknowledged still intellectually divisible, must still have parts into which they are divisible; and therefore be still discerpible? to this it is answered; That division into parts does not imply any discerpibility, because the parts conceived in one of these *minima Corporalia*, as I may so call them are rather Essential or Formal parts then integrall, and can no more actually be dissevered than sense and reason from the Soul of a man: For it is of the very essence of Matter to be divisible, but it is not at all included in the essence thereof, to be discerpible; and therefore where discerpibility failes, there is no necessity that divisibility should fail also: As for the trouble

ble of spurious sugestions or representations from the fancy, as if these perfect parvitudes, were round bodies, and that therefore there would be triangular intervals betwixt, void of matter; they are of no moment in this Case, she alwayes representing a discerpible magnitude instead of an indiscerpible one; wherefore she brings in false evidence, her testimony is to be rejected: Nay, if she could perplex the cause far worse, she was not to be heard; wherefore fancy being unable to exhibite the Object we consider, in its due advantages, for ought we know these perfect parvitudes may lie so close together, that they have no intervals betwixt: nay, it seems necessary to be so; for if there were any such intervals, they were capable of particles, lesse than these least of all, which is a contradiction in reason, and a thing utterly impossible.

But if we should gratifie Fancy so far as to Admit of these intervalls, the greatest absurdity would be, that we must admit an insensible vacuum, which no Faculty will be able ever to confute, but it is most rationall to admit none, and more consonant to our determination concerning these *minima Corporalia*, as the *Rosie Crucians* call them, whose largenesse is to be limited to the least real
touch

touch of either a *Globe* or *plaine*, or a *Cone* on a *plaine*, or a *Globe* on a *Globe*: if you conceive any reall touch leſſe then another, let that be the meaſure of theſe *Minute Realities* in matter, from whence it will follow, they muſt touch a whole ſide at once, and therefore can never leave any empty intervals; Nor can we Imagine any Anguloſityes or round protuberancies in a quantity infinitely little, more then we can in one infinitely great, as I have already declared in my book, called, *The Wiſe mans Crown*: I muſt confeſs a mans reaſon in this ſpeculation is mounted far beyond his imagination; but there being worſe intricacies in *Theories* acknowledged conſtantly to be true, it can be no prejudice to the preſent concluſion.

Thus have I not only ſaid, there is a *God*, *Angels* or *Meſſengers*, that wait upon the commands of *God* and his *Ideas*, but proved it alſo: and the *Idea* of a Spirit and its indiſcerpibility, as well in Centre as Circumference, as well in the primary as ſecondary ſubſtance thereof, to be a very conſiſtent and Congruous Notion, but before I can come to the *Harmony of the Macrocoſme or great world*, another property runs by me: that I obſerve to be ſelf Motion, which muſt of neceſſity be an Attribute of ſomething or other, for by ſelf motion I underſtand nothing elſe

else but self activity, which must appertain to a subject active of it self. Now what is simple Active of it self, can no more cease to be active then to Be; which is a signe that Matter is not Active of it self, because it is reducible to Rest:

Which is an Argument not only that self Activity belongs to a Spirit, but that there is such a thing as a Spirit in the world, from which Activity is communicated to Matter: And indeed if Matter as Matter had Motion, nothing would hold together but *Flints, Pebbles, middle Minerals, Adamants, Brasse, Iron, Silver, Gold*; yea this whole earth would suddenly melt into a thiner substance then the subtile Aire, or rather it never had been condensed together to this consistency we finde it: But this is to Anticipate my purpose of proving, that there are spirits existing in the world, that conduct the *Heavens, Stars, Planets, Men, Beasts* and all manner of living Creatures in their *motions, Beings* and *Actions*, &c.

It had been sufficient here to have asserted, That self Motion, or self Activity is as Conceivable to appertain to a spirit as body, which is plain at first sight to any man that appeals to his own faculties. Nor is it all to be scrupled at, that any thing should be al-
lowe

lowed to move it self; because our Adversaries that say, there is nothing but Matter in the world, must of necessity (as I have intimated already) confesse that this Matter moves it self, though it be very incongruous so to affirm; The congruity and possibility of self penetration in a created spirit is to be conceived, partly from the limitablenesse of the subject, and partly from the foregoing Attributes of indiscerpibility and self motion; for self penetration cannot belong to *God*, because it is impossible any thing should belong to him that implies imperfection, and self penetration cannot be without the lessening of the presence of that which does penetrate it self, or the implication that some parts of that essence are not so well as they may be, which is a contradiction in a Being, which is absolutely perfect. From the Attributes of indiscerpibility and self motion, to which you may add penetrability from the general *Idea* of a spirit, it is plain that such a spirit as we define, having the power of Motion upon the whole extent of its essence, may also determine this Motion, according to the property of its own nature: And therefore if it determine the motion of the exteriour parts inward, they would return inwards the Centre of essential

tial power; which they may easily doe without resistance, the whole subject being penetrable, and without damage, it being also indiscerpible;

From this self penetration we do not onely easily, but necessarily understand self-contraction and dilatation to arise; for this self moving substance, which we call a spirit cannot penetrate it self; but it must needs therewith contract it self; nor restore it self again to its former state; but it does thereby dilate it self; so that we need not at all insist upon these terms: That power which a spirit hath to penetrate Matter we may easily understand, if we consider a spirit onely as a substance, whose immediate property is Activity. For then it is not harder to imagine this active substance to pervade this or the other part of matter, then it is to conceive the pervading or dispreading of Motion it self therein.

The greatest difficulty is to fancy how this spirit, being so incorporeal can be able to move the matter, though it be in it, for it seems so subtle, that it will passe through, leaving no more footsteps of its being there, then the lightning does in the scabbard, though it may happily melt the sword, because it there finds resistance. But a spirit can
finde

find no resistance any where, the closest matter being easily penetrable & pervious to an incorporeal substance, the ground of this difficulty is founded upon the unreceivablenesse of any *Union* that can be betwixt the matter and a substance, that can so easily passe through it. For if we could but once imagine union betwixt Matter and a Spirit, the activity then of the Spirit would certainly have influence upon Matter, either for begetting or increasing, or directing the motion thereof. But notwithstanding the penetrability and easie passage of a Spirit through Matter, there is yet for all that a strong union betwixt them, and every whit as conceivable as betwixt the parts of Matter themselves, for what Glue or Cement holds the parts of hard matter in Stones and Mettals together, or, if you will, of what is absolutely hard, that has no pores or particles, but is one continued and perfectly homogeneous body, not onely to sense, but according to the exact *Idea* of Reason, what Cements holds together the parts of such a body as this? Certainly nothing but *immediate Union and Rest*: Now for Union there is no comparison betwixt that of matter with matter, and this of spirit with matter. For the first is onely superficiall; in this latter

ter the very inward parts are united point to point throughout; nor is there any fear it will not take hold, because it has a capacity of passing through: For if we admit an absolutely hard, solid body in the *World*, which let be A. in which let us conceive inward Superficies, suppose E. A. C. this Superficies, is so smooth as nothing can be conceived smoother;

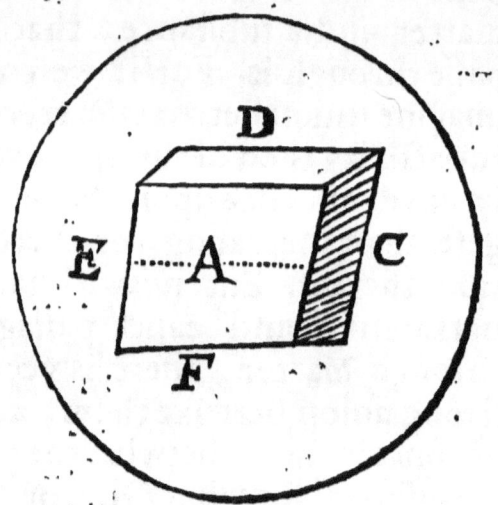

why does not therefore the upper E. D. C. slide upon the neather part E. F. C. upon the least motion imaginable, especially E. F. C. being supposed to be held fast, whilest the other is thrust against?

This facility therefore of one body passing upon another without any sticking, seeming as necessary to our fancy as a spirit passing through all bodies, without taking hold of them; it is plain that a firm union of spirits, and matter is very possible, though we cannot conceive the manner thereof. And

as

as for Rest, it is compitable alfo to this conjunction of Matter with Spirit, as well as of Matter with matter. For suppose the whole body A. moved with like swiftnesse in every part, the parts of A. then are according to that sense of rest, by which they would explain the Adhæsian of the parts of Matter one with another, truly quiescent.

So say I that in the union of matter with the spirit, the parts of the matter receiving from the spirit, just such a velocity of motion as the spirits exerts and no more; they both rest in firm union one with another. That which comes to passe even then, when there is far lesse immediate Union then we speak of; For if we do but lay a piece of Gold on our hand, provided our hand be not moved with a swifter motion then it communicates to the *gold*, nor the *gold* be pusht on faster then the swiftnesse of our hand: The *gold* and hand will most certainly retain their union and go together : So natural and easie it is to conceive, how a *spirit* may move a *body* without any more perplexity, or contradiction then is found in the union and motion of the parts of matter it self.

Chap.

Chap. IV.

Of the Harmony of the Macrocosme or great World: Of the Order and Nature of it; how the Sun, Moon and Stars receive their Light, and the Heavens their Motions; how they are guided in their several Spheres; and how by their mutual Presence, Absence and various Meetings, the visible Heavens receive the brightnesse of the Spiritual world, and this Earth the brightnesse of the visible Heavens.

NOw being come to behold the *Harmony* of the world; I say all musick consisteth in voice, in sound, and hearing: sound without aire cannot be audible, nor to be perceived by any sense, unlesse by accident; for the sight seeth it not, unlesse it be coloured, nor the ears unlesse sounding, nor the smell unlesse odoriferous, nor the taste unlesse it be sapid, nor the touch unlesse it be cold or hot, and so forth. Therefore though sound cannot be made without Aire, yet is not sound of the nature of aire, nor aire of the nature of sound; but aire is the body of the life of our sensitive spirit, and is not of the nature of any sensible object, but of a

more

more simple and higher vertue; but it is meet that the sensitive Soul should vivifie the aire joyned to it, and in the vivificated aire, which is joyned to the spirit, perceive the species of objects put forth into act, and this is done in the living aire, but in a subtile and Diaphanous, the visible species, in an ordinary aire the audable, in a more grosse aire the species of other senses are perceived.

The *Planets, Saturn, Mars*, and the *Moon* have more of the voice then of the *Harmony. Saturn* hath sad, hoarse, heavy and slow words and sounds, as it were pressed to the Centre; but *Mars* rough, sharp, threatning great and wrathfull words; the *Moon* observeth a mean betwixt these two; but *Jupiter, Sol, Venus* and *Mercury* does possesse harmonies; yet *Jupiter* hath grave, constant, fixed, sweet, merry and pleasant Consorts; *Sol* venerable, settled, pure and sweet, with a certain grace; but *Venus* lascivious, luxurious, delicate, voluptuous, dissolute and fluent; *Mercury* hath harmonies more remiss, and various, merry and pleasant with a certain boldnesse.

But the Tone of particulars and proportionated Consorts obeyeth the Nine Muses; *Jupiter* hath the grace of the Octave and also the Quinte, *viz.* the Diapason with the Diapente,

pente ; *Sol* obtains the melody of the Octave voice, *viz.* Diapason ; in like manner by fifteen Tones a *Diap..son* ; *Venus* keepeth the grace of the quinte or *Diapente.* *Mercury* hath *Diateffaron, viz* the grace of the Quarte. Moreover the Antients being content with four strings, as the number of *Elements*, accounted *Mercury* the Author of them, as *Facius Cardanus* reports, and by their base strings would resemble the *Earth*, by their *Pachypas* or middle the *Water*, by their Note *Diezeugmenon*, or *Hyperboleon* the *Fire* ; by the *Paranete* or *Synemmenon* or Treble the *Aire* ; but afterwards *Terpander* the *Lesbian* finding out the seventh string, equalled them to the number of Planets. Moreover, they that followed the number of the Elements, did affirm, that the four kindes of Musick doe agree to them, and also to the foure humours, and did think the Dorian Musick to be consonant to the *Water* and *Phlegme*, the *Phrigian* to *Choller* and *Fire*, the *Lydian* to *Blood* and *Aire*, the mixt *Lydian* to *Melancholly* and *Earth*.

Others respecting the Numbers and Vertues of the *Heavens*, have attributed the *Dorian* to the *Sun*, the *Phrigian* to *Mars*, the *Lydian* to *Jupiter*, the mixt *Lydian* to *Saturn*, the *Hyphrygian* to *Mercury*, the *Hypolidian* to *Venus*,

Venus, the *Hypodorian* to the *Moon*, the *Hypo mixed Lydian* to the *Fixed Stars*. Moreover these Modes of Musick are referred to the Muses, and the strings to the *Heavens*, but not in that order as I have declared concerning the *Nine Muses*, amongst our numbers and *Celestial Souls*. For *Thalia* hath no *Harmony*, although she be a beauty of Nature; therefore we ascribe her to a *silent Lady* that governs the *Earth*; but *Clyo* her sister with the *Moon* moves after the *Hypodorian* manner, the string *Proslambanomenos* or *arie*, *Calliope* and *Mercury* possesse the *Hypophrygian* manner, and the Chord, *Hypate Hypaton*, or B. Mi. *Terpsichore* with *Venus* the *Hypolydian* manner, and *Parahypote, Hypaton*: and for *Melpomene* and the *Dorian* manner with *Lyanos, Hypaton* or *D. Sol. Re*, are applied to the *Sun*, Mrs. *Erata* with *Mars* keep the *Phrygian* fashion, and the *Hypatemise*, E. la, mi. Madam *Euterpe*, *My Mistresse and Lady* loves the *Lydian* Musick, and *Pachyparemeson* agree with *Jupiter*; *Polymnia* and *Saturn* keep the mixt *Lydian* manner, and *Lychanos Meson D. Sol, Re*, to Madam *Urania* and the fixt Stars, the *Hypo* mixt *Lydian* Musick, and the string *Mese*, or A, le. mi. re. are ascribed as we finde them in this following Figure from the Hypothesis of Copernicus.

E   Who

The Harmony of the World.

Who here exactly teacheth the Revolutions of the Spheres, who beginning with the Primum Mobile, moves round in 36000. years, Saturn in 30. years, and Jupiter in 12. &c.

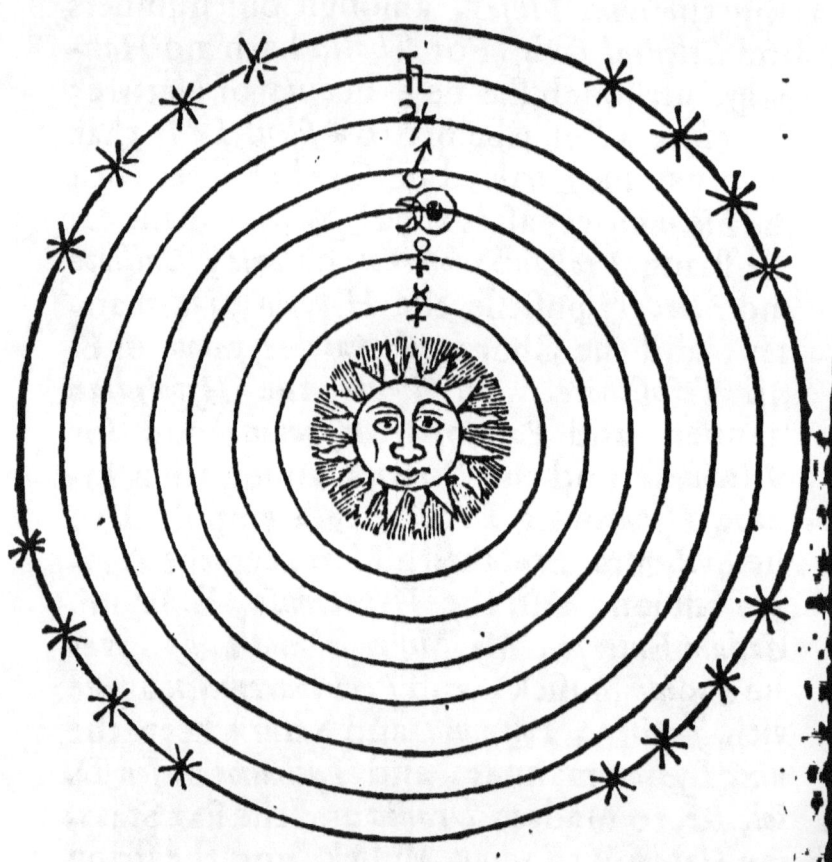

By this Figure I finde out the *Harmony* the *Heavens*, and their distance one from another, it is, and, it doth salve this *Phænomena*

Phænomena: For the space which is betwixt the Earth and the *Moon*, *viz*. an hundred twenty and six thousand *Italian* miles, maketh the interval of a Tone; but from the *Moon* to *Mercury* being half that space maketh half a Tone; and so much from *Mercury* to *Venus* maketh another half Tone:

But from thence to the *Sun*, as it were a threefold tone and a half, and makes Diapente, but from the *Moon* to the *Sun*, maketh a twofold diatessaron, with a half: again from the *Sun* to *Mars* is the same space as from the Earth to the *Moon*, making a tone; from thence to *Jupiter* half of the same, making half a tone; so much likewise from *Jupiter* to *Saturne*, constituting an half tone, from whence to the *Starry Firmament* is also the space of an halftone; Therefore there is from the *Sun* to the fixed stars a diatessaron distance of two tones & a half, but from the *Earth* a Diapason of six perfect Tones: Moreover also from the proportions of the Motions of the Planets amongst themselves, and with the eight Sphere resulteth the sweetest Harmony of all: For the proportion of the Motions of *Saturne* to *Jupiters* Motion is twofold and a half; of *Jupiter* to *Mars* a six fold proportion; of *Mars* to the *Sun, Venus* and *Mercury*; which in a manner finish their course in the same time, is a double proportion, their Motion to the *Moon* have a twelve fold proportion, but *Saturns* proportion to the *Starry Heaven* is a thousand and two hundred according to the *Hypothesis* of Sr. *Chr. Heydon, viz.* that the *Heaven* is moved contrary to the *Primum Mobile* in an hundred years one degree; therefore the proper motion of the *Moon* being more swift maketh a more acute sound then the *Starry firmament*, which is the slowest of all, and therefore causeth the more base sound;

But by the violent motion of the *Primum Mobile*, is the most swift and accute sound of all; but the violent Motion of the *Moon* is most slow and heavy, which proportion and reciprocation of motions yeilds a most pleasant Harmony; from hence there are not any Songs, Sounds, or Musicall Instruments more powerfull in moving mans affections or introducing impressions, then those which are composed of Numbers, Measures and Proportions, after the example of the *Heavens*; Also the *Harmony* of the *Elements* drawn forth from their basis and *Angles* I shall speak of in order: now between *Fire* and *Aire*, there is a double proportion in the

Ba

Basis, and one and a half in solid Angles, again in planets a double; there arising hence an Harmony of a double *Diapason*, and *Diapente*; betwixt the *Aire* and *Water*, the proportion in their basis is double, and one and a half; hence *Diapason* and *Diapente*, but in their Angles double: hence again *Diapason*.

But between *Water* and *Earth*, the proportion in the Basis, is three fold and a third part more; from hence ariseth *Diapason*, *Diapente*, *Diatessaron*; but in the Angle again constituting *Diapente*; betwixt *Earth* and *Fire* in the Basis, the proportion is one and a half making *Diapente*; but in the *Angles* double causing *Diapason*, but between fire and water, *Aire* and *Earth*; there is scarce any Consonancy, because they have a perfect contrariety in their Qualities, but they are united by the Intermediate *Element*, as you shall finde in the following discourse after we have proved this *Hypothesis*.

E 3   Chap V.

Chap. V.

Grounds proving the motion and harmony of the Heavens and Planets, to be by the Angels, that Rule and Conduct them, and not in their power to move themselves, or cast any light, influence, or virtue to one another.

First, I consider the transcendent Excellency of the Nature of God; who being according to the true *Idea* of him, an essence absolutely perfect, cannot possibly be Body, and consequently must be something incorporeal; and seeing that there is no contradiction in the *Idea* of a spirit in general, nor in any of those kinde of spirits which I have written of; (where the *Idea* of God were set down amongst the rest) and that in the very *Idea* of him, there is contayned the Reason of his existence, as you may see at large in my *Temple of Wisdome*, about the eighth Chapter; certainly if we finde any thing at all to be, we may safely conclude that he is much more   For there is nothing besides him, of which one can give a reason why it is, unlesse we suppose him to be the Author of it.

Wherefore

Wherefore though God be neither visible nor Tangible, yet his very *Idea* representing to our Intellectuall faculties the necessary reason of his existence, we are (though we had no other argument drawn from our senses) confidently to conclude, that he is the first mover and cause of all things, in this Harmonious world.

The second Ground is the ordinary *Phænomena* of nature, the most generall whereof is Motion. Now it seems to me demonstrable from hence, that there is some being in the world distinct from matter. For matter being of one simple homogenial nature, & not distinguishable by specificall differences, as the schools, it must have ever the very same Essentiall properties, and therefore of it self it must all of it be either without motion, or else be self moving, and that in such or such a tenor or measure of motion, there being no reason immaginable, why one part of the matter should move of it self, lefs then another; and therefore if there be any such thing, it can only arise from external impediment; now I say, if matter be utterly devoyd of Motion in it self, it is plain it has its motion from some other substance that is not matter, that is to say, a *Substance* Incorporeal. But if it be moved of it self, in such or such a measure, the effect here being an Emanative Effect, cannot possible faile to be wherever Matter is; especially, if there be no external impedement: And there is no impediment at all, but that the Terrestrial parts might regaine an Activity very nigh equall to the Ætheriall, or rather never have lost it

For if the *Planets* had but a Dividend of all the motion which themselves and the Sun and Stars, and all the *Ætherial* matter possess (the matter of the *Planets*, being so little in comparison of that of the *Sun, Stars* and *Æther*) the proportion of motion that will fall due to them, would be exceeding much above what they have; for it would be as if four or five poor men in a very rich and popular City should, by giving up that estate they have, in a Levelling way, get equall share with all the rest; wherefore every *Planet* could not faile of melting it self into little lesser, finer substance then the purest *Æther*, but they not doing so, it is a signe, they have not their Motion, Harmony, and Agitation, nor influence of themselves; and therefore rest content with what has extrinsically accrued to them, be it less or more.

But the Pugnacious, to evade the stroke of our *Dilemma*, will make any bold shift, and though

though they affront their own faculties in saying so, yet they will say and must say, that the *Planets, Heavens, Angels* and *Men* are without motion of themselves, although they will say in spite of me, that part of the matter is self moving.

But to this I Answer, that first, this Evasion of theirs is not so agreeable to experience, but so fair as either our sence or reason can reach, there is the same matter every where: For consider the subtle parts of matter discoverable here below, those which for their subtlety are invisible, and for their activity wonderfull; I mean those particles that cause that vehement agitation we feel in *Winds.* They in time loose their motion, and become of a *visible* vapours consistencie, and turn to *Clouds* then to *Snow* or *Rain*, after haply to *Ice* it self; but then in processe of time, first melted into Water, then exhaled into Vapours; after more firmly agitated, do become *Winde* again: And that we may not think that this reciprocation into motion and rest belongs only to *Terrestriall particles*; that the *Heavens* themselves be of the same matter, is apparent from the *Ejections* of *Comets* into one *Vortex*, (as you may read in the *Methodically Learned* Mathematician Mr. John Gadbury *his Book of* Prodigies,) and the

the perpetuall rising of those spots and Scum upon the face of the *Sun*.

But secondly, To returne what is still more pugnant: This matter that is self moved, in the impressing of motion upon other matter, either loose of its own motion, or reteyns it still intire, if the first, it may be dispoyled of all its motion: and so that whose immediate nature is to *Move* shall *Rest*, the entire cause of its motion still remaining *viz* it self: which is a plain contradiction, if the second, no meaner an inconvenience then this will follow, that the whole world had been turned into pure *Æther* by this time, if not into a perfect flame, or at least, will be in the conclusion, to the utter destruction of all Corporeall Consistencies, for, that these self moving parts of matter are of a Considerable copiousnesse, the events does testify, they having melted almost all the world already into *Suns*, *Starrs* and *Æther*, nothing remaining but *Planets* and *Comets* to be dissolved: which all put together scarce beare so great a proportion as a Cherry to the Ball of the Earth, wherefore so potent a principle of Motion, still adding new motion to matter, and no motion once communicated, being lost (for according to the Lawes of motion, no body looses any more motion than then it communicates to any other)it plainly follows, that either the world had been utterly burnt up ere now, or will be at the end of every seven thousand years, which is a lesse time to come than that which is past: let us passe to the Harmony of the Aspects of Starrs.

Chap. VI.

Of the Harmony of the Aspects of the Planets, and how they do transfer their received Light and Vertue downwards: of Intentions and Remissions by Configuration of Starrs: and how the Light of the Starrs passeth unto all parts, and the Aireall Spirits to us by them.

I Grant that in all Scituations the *Starrs* send forth their beams unto all the parts of *Heaven* and *Earth*, which they behold, as may be argued out of Sr. *Christopher Heydon*, in defence for *Astrology* and discourses by means whereof, the beams and lines of true motion in every two *Stars* do retaine a mutuall respect one to another, and so do evermore intercept some Arke of *Heaven*, and

concur

concur at some Angle of the Earth, which may seem to make an Aspect among themselves: yet neverthelesse all the Antient and Moderne *Astronomers* following nature for their guide, have heretofore regarded these few configurations only, being but five in all, namely, the *Conjunction, Sextile, Quartile,* and *Opposition*; amongst which although the first do not commonly go for an Aspect, because every Aspect is reputed a proportioned distance between two or more Starrs; yet neverthelesse seeing a certain position of the Starrs in the *Zodiack* is rather considered in this position, then any diversity of place, and that the enumeration of the Aspects ever beginneth from the Conjunction: Therefore as well in respect of this Analogy, as of the received use, it may not be secluded out of the number of Aspects, especially knowing that the Beames of the Starrs are as well extended upward and downward as obliquely & Collatterally; & by these beams are those *Idea's*, which originally proceed from God gradually imparted to the Aire, and from the air to the matter daily, by the help of the soul of the world, for the *Anima Mundi* hath in the fixed Stars her particular forms or Seminal Conceptions answerable to the *Ideas* of the Divine minde; of this you shall

shall be better satisfyed in the following discourse.

Now if any man desire to know my reasons, why I observe these distances and Arks assigned unto the Aspects, as of more vertue then any other, surely the answer is easy, seeing nature it self every where, both in the motions and effects of the heavenly bodies, as also in other Arithmeticall, and Geometricall respects, chiefly celebrateth these very proportions with a Singular prerogative, Nature hath as it were first allured us to observe the Aspects by speciall tokens or secret marks in the motion, and by them we know the Nature of the Native, in Body & Spirit.

Agrippa speaking hereof, thinketh they were first induced hereunto by observing the severall illuminations or ages of the *Moon*, for that when she is new, horned in her quarters, gibbosity and fullnesse, her formes are still changed at these proportioned spaces from the Sun.

Besides which, it is not to be passed in silence, which others have more particularly noted, then in her Annuall Revolution, she is still found about the *Trine* of her own place in the beginning of the former year.

Neither have other *Philosophers* failed to note, how Nature pointeth (as it were with a
fin-

finger) particularly unto every configuration; that we might observe how the *Angels Ascend* & *Descend*, & consider the motions of the other Planets. For thus *Avenroes* wittily affirmeth the two inferiour *Planets* in their stations to observe the Arke proper to a square Aspect. *Ptolomy* likewise with him as skilfully commendeth unto us the observation of the △ by the stations of the three superiour *planets*. But above all, it cannot be considered without deep admiration, how nature hath singularly nobilitated all the Aspects in the motions of *Saturn* and *Jupiter*; for as their Conjunctions are rare, and but once in twenty years; so hath nature evermore disposed these Conjunctions in the most memorable places of the *Zodiack*, that is onely in such signes as behold one another in an *equaliter*, Triangle inscribed; for between any two Conjunctions of *Saturn* and *Jupiter*, there are 19 *Ægyptian* years, 318. dayes and 13. houres, in which time those Planets are moved from the place of their Conjunction and Signes, and almost three degrees, which accesse of three degrees is the cause why after Conjunctions, they passe from one Triplicity to another, and one Triplicity continueth 198. equal years 265. dayes (the intercalary day of every four year omitted) and ten hours.

houres. But the Revolution of all the Triplicities is finifhed, but onely once in 794. equall years, 339. dayes, and 16. houres, or elfe in 724. *Julian* years, 133. dayes, 16. houres; the double commeth to 1588, which number of years they are thought to have refpected, that imagined the year 1588. from the birth of *our Lord and Saviour Jefus Chrift*, would have been fo fatall. From hence therefore it is, that not without caufe, they are called great Conjunctions; as you will finde by the great changes and cruell influence of them about the years 1663, 1664, 1665, 1666, 1667, 1668, 1669. thefe years are likely to be troublefome; but all lyeth in the power of Almighty God; I may not tell you what fhall particularly happen in the world, to *France* firft, &c.

They abide thus in one Triplicity almoft 200. years, and not finifhing all the Triplicities of the Zodiack in much leffer than 800. years; not having therefore reiterated all the Triplicities eight times fince the beginning of the world. Neither are the other Pofitions of the *planets* to be neglected: for if any man will take the pains to obferve when *Saturn* and *Jupiter* do behold one another with a Square or Oppofition Afpect, they fhall evidently perceive that they ftill

carry

carry such a regard unto the Signs or places of their precedent Conjunctions, as ever more they irrediate the one and the other with a Sextile, Quartile, Trine or Opposition Aspects: And now this shall suffice to shew how every thing receives the virtue, influence and nature of the Stars and Planets; and thus you see the reason why one hearb bears a white flower and another a red, &c. The corruption of the Ayre and Earth changes the colours and kindes of Plants, and their seminal forms; and these influences of the Stars send down several souls of Brutes, into various bodies, &c.

And now in a word, to confirm the same by their virtue and effects: First, The *Physitians* are taught by experience, that the Crisis of all sharpe diseases have a notorious and most memorable simpathy with all these five configurations of the *Moon*, to the place of her being in the beginning of the sicknesse: Thus also you see the Seas themselves in their Tides to dance as it were after the motion of the *Moon*, while their Spring and highest floods alwayes comes with her Conjunction and Opposition to the *Sun*, as their Neaps and lowest Tides doe likewise respect her Quarters; and as memorable a thing it is, that the Seas in their daily flowing and ebbing

ebbing upon every Coast, have still a constant respect onely to such *Azimuthal* circles as are in a *Quartile* positure when the Moon passeth by them, it is more manifest then that I need to insist upon it, that the Sun it self seemeth greatly to respect the *Quartile*, in that he moderateth the vicissitudes of foure quarters of the year by his ingresse into the four Æquinoctial and Tropical points.

But now to descend to other speculations more misticall then these, it is not amisse to begin with the Arithmeticall Observation, which the *Rosie Crucians* make of the Number of Signes agreeable to the Aspects; 1, 2. 3, 4. 6. answering in order to the *Conjunction*, *Sextile*, *Quartile*, *Trine*, and *Opposition*, for these numbers only, and none other, will devide the *Zodiack*, consisting of twelve signes, for which reason, they make them the only aliquate parts of a Circle. Thus also the Famous *Ptolomy* addeth not a little to the dignity of these irradiations, when he first observed the *Geometrical* proportion, which the subtenses of every of these Arks do retain in power to the Diameter of a Circle, as every man may read in the *Quadripartite*, others again, with no lesse subtlety, have observed, that amongst all Regular or ordinate figures that may be inscribed in a Circle, though

F   the

the same be infinite, there are none whose sides and Angles carry away the prerogative both at the Circumference and Center, but those whose sides and Angles are answerable to the subtenses and Arkes of their Aspects:

For thus amongst all ordinate Plains that may be inscribed, there are two whose sides joyned together have preheminence to take up a Semi-Circle, but only the *Hexagon, Quadrate*, and *Æquilaterall Triangle*, answering to the *Sextile, Quartile*, and *Trine*, irradiated the subtence thereof, of a *Sextile* Aspect, consisteth of two signes, joyned to the subtence of a *Trine*, composed of foure, being regular and æquilater, take up six signes which is a compleat semicircle; in like manner the sides of a quadrate inscribed, subtending three signs, twice reckoned, do employ likewise the Mediety of a Circle, and what those Figures are beforesaid to performe, either doubled or joyned together, may also be truly ascribed unto the opposite aspect by it self, for that the Diametrall Line, which passeth from the place of Conjunction to the opposite point, divideth a *Circle into two equal parts, the like whereof cannot be found in any other inscripts*. For example, the side of a Rule

Pentago

Pentagon subtended 72, degr. of an Octagon, but 45. the remainder of which Arks, *viz.* 108 and 135. gr. are not subtended by the sides of any ordinate figure.

We will in order shew you the *Harmony* of *Beams*, and how the *Seminall formes*, *Soules* of *Brutes*, *Humane Soules*, and *Spirit* of *Nature* glides down by them; Now the subtenses of these Aspects be the same with the sides of the fore-remembred inscripts, and do onely therefore take up the circumference of a Circle: So it is evident, that the angles at which they concur, be the same wherewith the ordinate plains take up the whole space about the Centre; for if we consider the angle of a Sextile at the Earth, it is all one with that of an equilater triangle, consisting of 60. gr. and containeth $\frac{2}{3}$ of a right angle, but six times $\frac{2}{3}$ of a right angle makes four right angles; where six Sextiles equal to six equilater Triangles fill the whol space about a Point, which is equall to four right angles.

Secondly, Every angle of a Quartile is a right angle, and all one with the angle of rectangle Quadrilator figure; wherefore foure of them fill a whole space, and this is the reason that every Man, Woman, Monkey, Ape, Mare-man, Mare-maid, and all other living Creatures differ one from another;

You seldome see two things of any kinde in the world a like one another, that you could not know them if they stood before you; Observe how that there is nothing upon the land, but it is also in the waters, of all manner of living Creatures, the reason proceeds from the Radiation of Stars, &c. but to my purpose.

Thirdly, The angle which two Stars in a Trine make at the Centre of the world, is measured by an angle of 120. gr. and so equall to the angle of a regular *Hexagon*, consisting of a right angle, and of $\frac{1}{3}$ of a right angle; and therefore taken three times maketh four right angles: Wherefore three equilater *Hexagons*, or three Trine Aspects, doe also fill the whole space about the Centre: To which we may not improperly add the Opposite Aspect, consisting of two right angles, and therefore doubled, shall perform the like Office with the rest.

Any other figure of many angles, however ioyned together at the angles, shall either want of four Angles or exceed them; for example, the angle of *Pentagon* containeth a right angle and $\frac{1}{5}$ more; wherefore three such angles placed about a point, shall fall short of four right angles by $\frac{2}{5}$ of a right angle, as on the other side; four such angles
shall

shall exceed four right Angles ¼.

These speculations therefore considered, it were senseless to imagine, that Nature hath so many wayes honoured these irradiations of the Stars in vain, and admonished us to a special regard of them by so many rare and secret Observations both in the motions of the Planets (as you heard before) and also in their effects and proportions; if they were not indued with more virtue than others; wherefore it hath no less exercised the learned Dr. *Ward*, Mr. *Tho. Heydon*, Mr. *More*, and *Eugenius Theodidactus*, to finde out the reason, why these few Configurations, selected out of an infinite number, should be indued with such eminent efficacy. Neither as yet hath any reason been invented, with more applause for the probability thereof, then these proportions; *The learned Knight*, Sr. *Christopher Heydon*, demonstrates whereof, the Aspects are before shewed to consist, and they are the same which are found in *Harmonical Concords*.

For which cause, it is also thought no less probable, that the light of the Stars in these proportioned distances, should powerfully affect the matter of sublunary things, then that the like Geometrical Symmetry in sounds and voices should passionately stir up

F 3 the

the sense of the hearer. For to confesse the truth, so hath the admired providence of Nature ordained throughout all her works, that where due proportion is not wanting, there she never faileth to endue all her effects with such height of perfection, that the same becomes evident to the eye of every man: And from hence it is even in Artificial compositions also, as in Medicines; we know those onely to be most kinde and soveraign which observe a competent symmetry or temperature of the Active and passive qualities; with good likelihood therefore, and appearance of truth do most of the learned with *Hobs*, Dr. *Barlow* of *Queens*, Master *More*, and Mr. *Fisk*, resolve the onely cause of this efficacy from *Harmonicall proportion*.

And more clearly to expresse this similitude or affinity between the proportions of Aspects, and the like distances observed in the Musical Concords; we must understand (besides what we have said before) that all *harmony* whatsoever springeth originally from three such terms of numbers, as respect each other in such sort, that still their differences retain the same proportion that is found between the extreams. For example, in these three numbers 6, 4, 3. (answerable to the signes of the ☍, △, & □ configurations)

The Harmony of the World.

figurations) here it is evident, if we compare the extreams with the mean, that two shall be the difference betwixt six; the first and four the second, and three the third number.

But two is double in proportion to one, therefore six the first number respecteth three, the third number with the like proportion. The Analogie of which proportions, as is before remembred, is found to be the fountain of all musick (as you heard before) rising originally from these three simple concording distances, which by the Musitians are called (as I have writen before) namely, Diapente, consisting of a sesquialter proportion, as six to four; or which is all one of three to two Diatessaron of a. *sesquitertia*, as foure to three; And lastly, Diapason consisted of a double proportion, as six to three, or two to one; and is, as much in value, as both the two first distances and proportions put together.

For a *Sesquilater* added to a *sesquitertia*, according to the art of Proportions, doe produce a Diapason, or double proportion; such as is found between the former extreams compared together, viz. six and three, and in like manner, by comparing the Diapason with both these his parts, that is, with the
sesquilater

sesquialter and *sesquitertia*, according to the usuall manner of supputating proportions, we are brought to the two other compounded, or imperfect concords, so constituting the five first and natural distances in Harmonical mixture, which afterwards, as they be diversly mixed between themselves, produce infinite variety of all kinde of melody.

After the same manner fareth it with the light and influence of Heaven: For although anciently there be but five irradiations observed, as most apt to action, namely, the ☌, ☍, △, ☐, & ✶; yet neverthelesse there is nothing more sure, then that by the Harmonical mixture of these proportioned beams, the generation and corruption of all living things in the Aire, Earth, and Water, *viz.* Men, Beasts, Fowle, Fishes, and creeping things and Plants of this mortal world, are infinitely varied; For Children cry as soon as they are born, &c. And you see in several forms and species according to their kindes great differences; wherefore as the force of all Harmony, so likewise the effectual reason of all action in the influence of the stars, is properly deduced from the foresaid semmetry of these distances; And therefore more fully to illustrate, that the angles of the Aspects, compared between themselves,

con-

concur with these Harmonies of Musick, it will be no hard matter, if that which hath been often repeated before be called to minde.

As that first, the Stars in an Opposite or Diametral Aspect are disjoyned by the space of two right angles, which are measured with the Ark of six signes, or 180. degrees of circumference; and that the Trine consisting of four signes, or 120. degrees is in value one right angle and ⅓ of a right angle: also that the Quartile taketh up one intire right angle, and is subtended with the Ark of three signes, or 90. degrees. And lastly, that the Sextile is constituted but of two signes, or 60. gr. which is ⅔ of a right angle; which being thus, if we now so compare the two right angles of the Opposition taken together with the angles of the rest of the Aspects; if either the Trine be placed between the Opposition and the Quartile, or the Quartile between the Opposition and the Sextile; you shall finde either way three numbers, which admit all the laws of harmonical proportions; Sr. *Christopher Heydon* hath so well demonstrated this, that I need not further explain my minde; *For his Hypothesis salves this Phænomena*; where to let the rest passe, as plain enough of it self, by that

which

which is written before: You are further to note, that the Opposition compared with the Sextile, hath a triple proportion to the same, compounded of a double and sesquialter proportion, as Diapente with Diapason in Musick is, and so is found no simple or perfect Aspect: but exactly answerable to B. flat; the first imperfect or compounded concord in Musick being a sixth from G. sol, re, ut, which neverthelesse in some respects is after a sort esteemed perfect; because it useth the same division compared to D. sol, re, that the perfect concords do; For it is half a fifth, and scituate in the middle between Γ ut and D. sol, re, as also the Sextile compared with the Trine is a just half thereof, which before hath been shewed in a sesquilater proportion to the Opposition, as D. sol. re is to Γ ut, and therefore exactly agreeable to a Diapente in Musick, which the rather I here note, because you will have some use thereof afterward in observing, how spirits or Genii slip down by other beams, not formerly observed, and these our best Astronomers and Mr. *John Gadbury*, Mr. *Wing*, marke new Aspects. And thus much shall shortly serve for the *Theory* or *Philosophicall* speculation of them that ascribe to the efficacy of these iradiations to the *Harmonicall proportion*, which

is

is found between them: Wherefore *seeing these Learned Gentlemen admit them into Astrology*, they shall then carry the same mutual respect one towards another, which the aforesaid *Harmonicall concords* do retaine between themselves, what wonder is it if nature in her operations, as well by *Lights* as by sounds admitted no other Symmetry, but that which is derived from these proportions, rejecting all other as irrationall and discordent.

I shall next lay down some Reasons, why the aforesaid *Harmonicall* proportions are so effectuall, drawn from the Symmetry of the world, being the same that is found between the five regular bodies inscribed one within another, why in the infinite variety of sounds and lights, these only should consent most sweetly in musick, sending down souls so merily to the *Moon*, and from thence they come down sadly to the belly and Matrix of the *Earth* in prolific spirited *Winds* and *Waters*, and be effectual in the operations of nature: Neither hath any man herein endeavoured with more probability to give satisfaction unto the learned then *Des Cartes*, who having wittily laboured to demonstrate, that God in the creation of the world hath observed the same proportion in the magnitude

tude and distance of the *heavenly spheres*, which is found in the regular *Solides*, which (as *Geometry* teacheth) have their originall from the ordinate plains: In the end concludeth with good propability, that the *Heavenly* motions shall then consent sweetly, and Co-operate strongly together, when the nature of these sublunary things, indued (as he supposeth) with a sensitive or knowing faculty, apprehendeth the beams of the *Stars* to observe that respect in their concurrence at the Center of the *Earth*, which answereth unto the ordinate Plains, from whence the Regularity of these proportions is derived, as the impressed Characters of that *Symmetry*, which God is said to have used in the Creation of the world it self.

So supposing, that as often as the nature of any thing meeteth with these proportions, it exerciseth it self as it were by *The Idea*, which it alwayes retayneth, and that in such sort, as what it doth but ordinarily and slackly at other times, it performeth now much more effectually, and as it were with extraordinary diligence: Nor (saith) Sr. *Christopher Heydon*) that these proportions work any thing of their own vertue, but of their *Idea's*; for in musick it is neither the sounds, neither the proportion of the concords,

ords, that work any thing of themselves, or beget any delightfull humour in a man, but he *Genius* approaching to the Instruments of sense first, carrieth the sounds inwardly and entertayning it, there valueth their proportions: and (finding the same good and *Geometricall*) lastly exhiliratech it self, and moveth the body, wherein it is as with in Object, wherein it taketh delight.

I will as perspicuously as I can deliver that which my self have further considered, as the reason why these beams should be more effectual than others, to let down and shed some secret influx of spirit; And you must know, that there is no difference between the *Stars* and their *Orbes*, but that the *Star* is *Densior pars ejusdem*, and as the *Stars* differ one from another in motion, magnitude, colour and vertue, so likewise those parts of *Heaven*, not onely admit, but send down the like variety of nature and qualities; The Conjunction and Opposition are the most potent and powerfull Configurations of all others, in their union of Beams, as is evident in this figure; where you see the Beams as well incident as reflected to be united, according to Sr. *Chr. Heydons* Hypothesis, let *A.* be in Conjunction here with *B.* it is first manifest, that all the Beams flowing from

G.

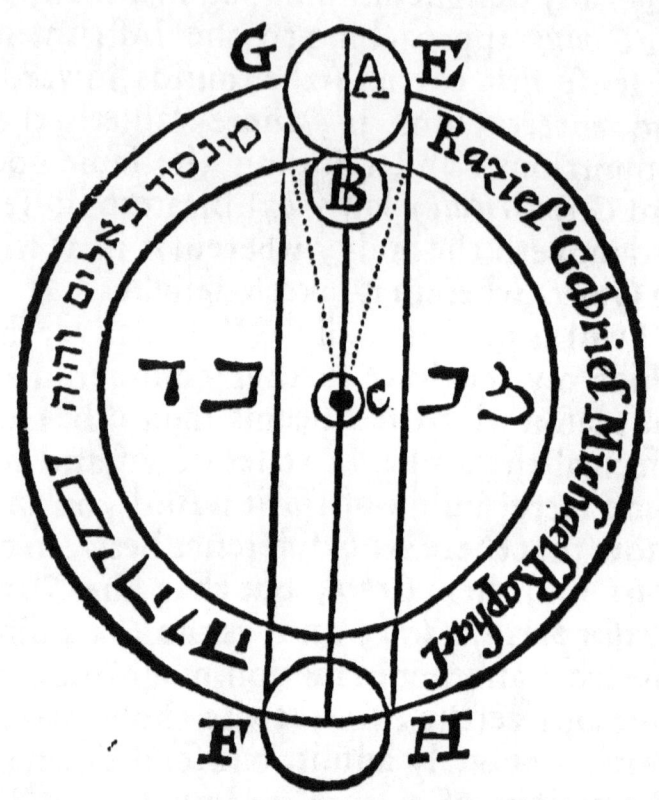

G. and E. the points of touch in the circumference of *A* shall unite themselves with the Beams that are sent from *B*. to *C*; the Centre of the world: Secondly, you are also to observe, that in this case onely, the Beams onely of *A. C.* or *B. C.* comming from the Centre of the *Stars*, reflecteth
into

into it self, as being onely perpendicular: Whereas those Beams which are sent from the points *E.* and *G.* make an acute angle at *C.* and do therefore reflect the one into the other at equal angles, as *G. C.* reflecteth from *C.* to *E.* and *E. C.* from *C.* to *G.* Last of all, the *harmony* that hapneth in Opposition, is manifest without more circumstance, where the Beams sent from the opposite points make but one streight line, as *G. F.* and *E. H.* in this Figure; except in cases where the Earth is bigger than the Star in Opposition, for there without latitude, the union of their beams must needs be hindred by interposition of the Earth; for which cause it is especially here to be remembred in the Conjunction of the two inferiour Planets with the *Sun*: That if this happen in the *Apogæon* of their *Epicycles*, their Conjunction shall not be of that efficacy or force, as when they are in *Perigæo*; because according to the *Hypothesis* of L. *Verulam*, they being above the *sun*, and the *sun* much bigger then they; the *sun* shall return all their beams to themselves from the Earth; so that their union by this means shall be interrupted and frustrate.

In like manner, in my Contemplation for help in the Configuration of the Sextile and Trine;

trine; I found that which did resonably give me contentment by discourse with Mr. *Tubb* the Astrologicall Fencer, because in the concurrence of their Beams at the Earth, I found a mutual reflection of the one into the other; and so an union by reflection.

The Genii that send down the influences are written in the outmost circle of all, and let

let us now admit *A. B. C.* to be three Stars; *A.* and *B.* in a Sextile Configuration; *A. C.* in a Trine; then for so much as *B. F.* the Beam incident of the Sextile, falleth obliquely in respect of *A. F.* and maketh an acute Angle therewith, it is evident to those that have any mean understanding in the Opticks, that *B. F.* shall reflect to *C.* and so be united to *C. F.* the incident of the Star *C.* which is in a Trine Configuration with *A.* as also *C. F.* shall for the same reason reflect to the Star in *B.* and be likewise united with *B. F* the incident of the Star at *B.* Behold here by the way, the grounds of that familiarity which *Phroates* the Indian Prince, noteth in these Arks of Heaven, when he considereth the Position apt for the *Aphæta* of life, or the Houses of the Figure; and thus far have I pursued the Harmony and vertue, which is found in the Aspects: But when I come to consider of the Quartile, whose Beams onely cut each other *ad angulos rectos*, and so reflect into themselves; after much deliberation with my self, finding all aid of the Opticks to faile, I was forced with *Severinus* to say, *Ingenuè fatebimur causam talis effectus nos demonstrare non posse: Id tamen verissimum esse tam diuturna observatione Compertum habemus, ut ea de re dubitare puderet.* Wherefore

Wherefore recounting with my self some o[f]
those speculations before remembred, an[d]
specially that Theorem of *Archimedes*, whic[h]
prove the angles of the Sextile, Quartile an[d]
Trine to be onely proportionable in takin[g]
up the Centre of the World; the more
consider thereof the more I find my self confirmed; that the myftery or secret of thef[e]
Configurations, is drawn from the *Element
of Spirits*, and reft chiefly in this, that thef[e]
onely irradiations, and those that are derived from these, are proportional unto al[l]
partile matter, and therefore more effectual

For that these Irradiations onely are every way proportionable is before proved,
whether you respect the taking up of the circumference, the power and proportion o[f]
their subtenses unto the Diameter; or laftly,
and principally, the occupying of place a[t]
the Centre of the world; which preroga-
tives seeing no other Arks, Subtenses or Angles do enjoy: Therefore I conclude thef[e]
above all others to be proportional unto th[e]
whole Syfteme of the world; for that is truly said proportionable, which is neither defective interrupted, nor redoundant; bu[t]
such are the Arkes, Subtenses and Angles o[f]
those Irradiations, and none other: *Ergo*,
These and none other are proportionable.
Now

Now as that which is defective, and wanteth proportion, leaveth the Action fruftrate, and without Effect.

So that which on the other fide offendeth in excefse, muft incur the contrary fault, and over charge that which either Nature or Art intendeth; whereby of neceffity it will follow, that there being no defect, nor excefse, but an equal and juft mixture of the influence of the *Stars* in thefe irradiations; thefe onely fhall be apt and convenient to produce agreeable effect in the matter of all *fublunary* things. For it fareth in thefe *Effects*, which are produced by the mixture of *Ethe-rial Fire*, *Idea's* and *Anima Mundi*: when their light and influence comes into the *aire*, as with the *Chymicall Doctors* in their opera-tions, where the defect of heat produceth nothing: as on the other fide, excefse doth either by fublimation, eruption, vitrification, breaking the veffel and the like, deftroy the work.

And to make it yet clearer, how the beams of any *Starr* do proportionally take up the centre of the world, whereas, in that which went before, I have only fhewed, how the joints of thofe ordinate plaines, whereunto thefe configurations have been compared, often reiterated, do take up place; I will fet forth

forth next, how the beams of any two Stars in any of the former configurations shall take up more space, then that which is comprehended between their incidents or beams of true motion; and how by their beams, either incident reflected, or opposite, they do possesse, and take up the whole centre of the world

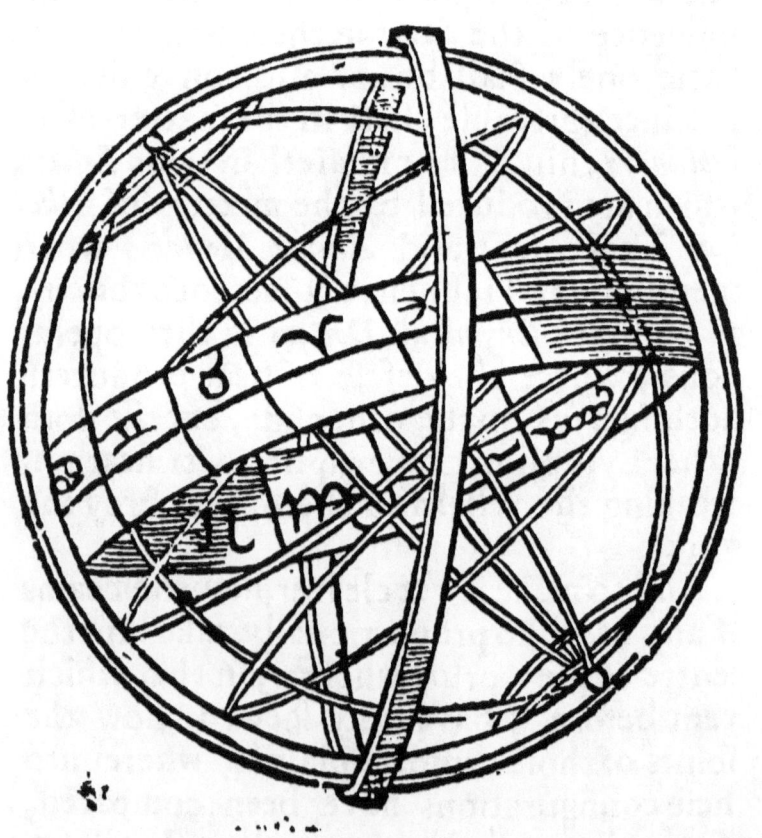

at an instant with proportionable angles, for evident demonstration whereof (as our manner is) is concerning Conjunction and Opposition (whose force rather tendeth upon union then proportion,) I need no further labour, then to referr the Gentlemen, to the view of the last figure but one, where they may see the united beams of such Stars as are in Conjunction and Opposition to surround the center, and all elementary matter whatsoever subject unto the *Actions of heaven, and the ten lights that stand upon the eternal, rich Firy Tapestry, spread under the throne of God and the Idea's of his Divine Mind.*

And so for the Quartile, whose beams incident and opposite, traverse the centre of the world at foure right angles viz. A F. G. G. F. I. A. F. H. and H. F. I. seeing foure points of a rectangle quadrilater figure hath been before proved to imploy place; I likewise need no other proof then the Gentlemen will in the last figure, consider how these foure right angles move by one quartile and take up the centre of the world. But concerning the Trine or Sextile, although the like be evident enough to any of mean skill, yet neverthelesse there are some other speculations which require a word or two more, for in the last figure suppose two starrs A. and
G 3   B.

B. Irradiate the earth with their Sextile beams, by various *Spirits* or *Genii* according to the place of Heaven; from whence these Aspects are darted, for you shall know the *Genii* may vary oftener then the wind and weather, and although it be true, that by the protracting of the opposite Beam from F. to D, the centre of the whole world seemeth used with proportionable angles B. F. A. being subtended by the ark of 60. which is before declared to be the angle of an ordinate æquilater triangle, and so leaveth the outward angle B. F. I. equall to the Angle of an ordinate *Hexagon*, subtended hereby the ark, 120, which is the ark of a Trine; the like being also understood of the angles made by the opposite beams adverticem, yet neverthelesse you are here further to consider, how the incident Beam of B. viz. B. F. reflecteth unto C. and so taketh up the whole semicircle A. B. C I. with three sextiles, viz. A. F. B. B. F. C. and C. F. I. In like manner, if you consider C. to be in a triangular Configuration with A. you see that as the opposite beame of A. viz. F. I. maketh a Sextile with the incident beame of a Starr at C. viz. C. F.

So *C. F.* being the beam incident of the Star *C.* **reflecteth** also to the point *B.* and so maketh

maketh the same three Sextiles, wherewith the whole Semicircle is taken up, as is before demonstrated: Wherefore this may satisfie the indifferent, how any two stars in any of these Configurations doe proportionally possesse the whole Centre of the world in the same moment without reiterating the same angle: Some able Artists have added unto these former Aspects three more viz *Quintile* consisting of 72. degr. the *Biquintile* of 144. deg. and the *Sesquiquadrate* of 135. degr. so making eight Configurations answerable to the eight Consonant stops in a *Monochord*: Neither dare I for my part contradict these new additions, For having made triall as well in the speculations of the weather and meteors, as in the accidents of *Nativities*, I dare boldly affirme, that there have divers events and effects concurred with these new configurations, for which without these Considerations, you can finde as yet no reason for this their Observation.

For as in *Musick* there be but three perfect concords, viz. the diapason, diapente, and diatessaron: so in the *Harmony* of the *Beams*, by which the *Genii* come down, there are but three perfect aspects answerable to the *Harmony* of the *Heavens*, *Spheres and Planets*,
Namely,

namely the opposition, the trine, & the quartile, the sextile being accounted, and so proved, to be but an imperfect Aspect answering exactly to B. flat, the first among the imperfect or compounded concords; wherfore considering that the first three perfect concords are found to have their perfect aspects answerable unto them, and that B. flat being an imperfect aspect, this made some *Gentlemen* suspect that the *Harmonical proportions* conteyned in the same *Monochord* might also have their aspects *viz.* the Quintile, Biquintile, and sesquiquadrate answerable unto them; and thus have I hunted through the heavens and traced the *Idea's* or *lights* of God through the *Sun*, and followed the *Genii* from their *Limbus*, a *sphære of pure etherial Fire*, through the *Moon and Aire* to the prepared matter of the Earth, in which God hath ordained to incorporate them, and now let no man therefore take occasion to callumniate Astrology, because a Gold chaine drew *William Lilly* to flatter the King of *Sweden, &c.* I intend not in this place to Apologize for that noble and admired Art: But to demonstrate the *Harmony* of the Macrocosme and Microcosme; thus I have past cleerly through the *Harmony* of the *Beames* or influence of the *lights* and *aspects* of the *planets*; and here I come

come to unite the *Genius* to the *body, &c.* but first I shall shew you the differences of *Genii.*

Chap. VII.

Of Seminal forms, *of* Souls of Brutes; *of the* soul of Man, *and how they differ in Nature one from another, and how the soule of a man differs from an Angel.*

Having now followed the *Genii* to the *Earth*; I shall enumerate *four kindes of them, viz.* The λογοι σπερματικοι, or *seminal forms*, the *soules of brutes*, the *Humane soule*, and that *Genius* or *spirit* which actuates or informs the *vehicles* of *Angels*. For I look upon *Angels* to be as truly a compound being, consisting of *Genius* and *Body*, as that of men and brutes: Their existence I shall not now go about to prove, for I have done that already in my Book, *The Temple of Wisdome*: My present designe is to demonstrate to you the *Harmony* of the *Macrocosme*, & *Microcosme* & how the

the *soul* of the one enters into the body of the other; and the difference of *Genii*; and to expound or define the notion of these things, so far forth as is needfull for the evincing that they are the *Ideas* or notions of things which imply no contradiction or impossibility in their Conception; which will be very easy for us to performe: the chief difficulty lying in that more generall *Idea* of a *Spirit, &c.*

Now this generall *Idea* can be contracted into kindes by no other difference then such as may be called peculiar powers or properties belonging to one Spirit and excluded from another, from whence it will follow, that if we describe these severall kinds of *Genii* by immediate and intrinsecall properties, we have given as good definitions of them as any one can give of any thing in the World.

I will begin with what is most Simple, the *Seminall formes of things*, which for the present deciding, nothing of their existence according to their *Idea Possibilis*, we define; *a seminal form is a created spirit, organizing duely prepared matter into life, and vegetation proper to this or the other kind of Plant*, it is beyond my imagination what can be excepted against this description, containing nothing but what is
very

very coherent and intelligible, for in that it is a spirit, it can move matter intrinsecally, or at least direct the motion thereof: But in that it is not an omnipotent spirit, but finite and created; its power might well be restrained to duely prepared matter, both for vitall union and motion; he that hath made these particular *spirits*, varying their faculties of vitall union according to the diversity of the preparation of matter, & so limiting the whole comprehension of them all, that none of them may be able to be vitally joyned with any matter whatsoever, and the same first cause of all things, that gives them a power of uniting with, and moving of, *matter duely prepared*; may also set such laws to this motion, that when it lights on matter fit for it, it will produce such and such a plant, *viz.* it will shape the matter into such figure, colour and other properties, as we discover in them by our senses; this is the first degree of particular life in the world, if there be any purely of this degree particular; but now as *Plato* has somewhere noted, the essences of things are like numbers, whose species are changed by adding or taking away an unite

Add therefore another intrincicall power to this of *vegetation, viz. sensation*, and it becomes

comes the *Genius* of a Br**[blot]** Beast. For in truth the bare substance it self is not to be computed in explicite knowledge, it being utterly in it self unconceiveable; and therefore, I will only reckon upon the powers, *A subject therefore from whence is both vegetation and sensation is the generall Idea of the soule of a Beast,* which is distributed into a number of kindes(as you shall see in the next chapter all in order) the effect of every intrinsical power being discernible in the constant shape and properties of every distinct kinde of brute creatures.

If we add to *vegetation* and *sensation reason* properly so called, we have then a setled *Idea* of the *Genius* of *man*, which I shall more compleatly describe thus, *A created spirit or Genius indued with sense and reason, and a power of organizing terrestriall Matter into humane shape by vitall union therewith, and herein* alone, I conceive does the *Genius* or *Soul* of an *Angell* differ, (for I take the boldnesse to call that soul, whatever it is, that has a power of vitally actuating the matter) differs from the *Genius* of a *man* in that the *Genius* of an *Angel* may vitally actuate *an aireal* or *æthereal body,* but cannot be borne into this world in a *Terrestriall one.*

An *Angelicall soul* is very intelligibly described

The Harmony of the World. 93

scribed thus, *A created spirit indued with reason, sensation and a power of being vitally united with, and actuating of a body of aire or æther only, which power over an aëreal or æthereal body*, is very easily to be understood by my *Wise mans Crown*, in the third Chapter; for it being there made good, that union with matter is not incompetible to a *Genius*, and consequently not moving of it, nor that kinde of motion in a *Spirit* which we call contraction and dilatation; these powers if carefully considered will necessarily infer the possibility of the actuation and union of an *Angelical Genius*, with an *Ætherial* or *aiery body*: *Plato* writes of other *Orders* of *Spirits*, or *Immateriall Substances*, as the Νόες and Ἐυάδες, But there being more subtelty then either usefullness or assurance in such like speculations, I shall passe them over at this time; having already irrefutably made good, that there is no incongruity, nor incompossibility comprised in the *Idea of a spirit*, or incorporeal substance.

But there is yet another way of inferring the same, & it is the argument of *Honest Paracelsus*, whereby he would conclude, that there is *de facto*, a substance in us distinct from matter *viz*. our own minde. For every reall affection of property being the mode of
some

some substance or other, and reall modes being unconceivable without their subjects; he inferrs that, seeing we can doubt whether there be any such thing as *body* in the *World*; (by which doubting we seclude Cogitation from body) there must be some other substance distinct from the body, to which cogitation belongs, but I must confess this argument will not reach home to *Paracelsus* his purpose, who would prove in man a substance distinct from his body; for being there may be modes common to more subjects then one, and this of Cogitation, may be pretended to be such as is competible as well to substance corporeall as incorporeall, it may be conceived apart from either though not from both. And therefore his argument does not prove that that which does think or perceive, is a substance distinct from our body, but only that there may be such a substance, which has the power of thinking or perceiving, which yet is not a body: And this was argued before Sr. *Ralph Freeman* Knight, &c. by Mr. *Thomas Heydon* and my self, who for fashion sake would needs say somthing syllogistically; but truth needs no Crutches. For it being impossible that there should be any reall mode, which is in no subject, and I clearly conceiving cogitation

tation independent, for exiſtence on corporeal ſubſtance; it is neceſſary, that there may be ſome other ſubſtance on which it may depend: which muſt needs be a ſubſtance incorporeall. And thus I have ſhewed you the differences of Genii; and now I ſhall demonſtrate how God by his Idea's gives life and vertue to all things in the world:

Chap. VIII.

How different vertues are infuſed into ſeverall kinds of things, by the influence of the heavens, Starrs and Planets.

I Might eaſily decline this Controverſie, by pleading onely, that the entrance of the *Soul* into the *Body*, ſuppoſing her pre-exiſtence, is as intelligible as in thoſe other two wayes, of Creation and Traduction. For how this newly *Created ſoule is infuſed by God*, no man knows, nor how? If it be traducted from the Parents, both their ſouls contribute to their making up a new one; For if
there

there be dicifion of part of the foule of the Male, in the injection of his feed into the Matrix of the Female, and part of the Female foule to joyn with that of the Males; befides that the decifion of thefe parts of their foules, makes the foule a difcerpible effence, it is unconceivable how thefe two parts fhould make up one foule for the Infant; A thing rediculous at firft view: But if there be no decifion of any parts of the *Soul*, and yet the *Soul* of the Parent be the caufe of the foul of the Childe, it is perfectly an act of Creation; a thing that all fober men conclude incompetable to any particular Creature. It is therefore plainly unintelligible, how any foul fhould paffe from the Parents into the body of the feed of the *Fætus*, to actuate and inform it; but that all inferiour bodies, are exemplified by the fuperiour *Idea's* or *Genii*: Now we define an *Idea* to be a form above bodies, fouls, minds, and to be but one fimple, pure, immutable, indivifible, incorporeal and eternal, and that the nature of all *Idea's* is the fame.

Now all *Idea's* proceed from *God*, and are diftinguifhed amongft themfelves by fome Relative confideration; leaft whatfoever is in the world fhould be but one thing without any variety, and that they agree in
effence;

essence; least God should be a Compound Substance. In the second place (to be very serious) we place them in the very intelligible it self, *in the soul of the world*, differing the one from the other by absolute forms; so that all the *Idea's* in God indeed are but one form; but in the *Anima Mundi* they are many: they are placed in the minde of all other things, whether they be joyned to the body, or separated from the body, by a certain participation; and now by degrees are distinguished more and more; we place them in Nature, as certain small seed of forms infused by the *Idea's*: And lastly, we place them in matter as shadows. Here unto may be added, that in the soule of the world, there be as many seminal forms of things, as *Idea's* in the minde of God.

Now again by these forms, she did in the Heavens, in the Element of Spirits above the Stars, frame to her self shapes also, and stamped upon all these some properties; on these stars therefore shapes and properties, and all vertues of inferiour species, as also their properties depend; so that every species hath its celestial shape or figure that is suitable to it; from which also proceeds a wonderfull power of operating, which proper gift, it receives from its own *Idea*, through

98 *The Harmony of the World.*

the seminal forms of the *anima mundi*: For *Idea*'s are not onely essential causes of every species, but are also the causes of every vertue, which is in the species; such as have a certain and sure foundation not fortuitous nor casual, but efficacious, powerfull and sufficient, doing nothing in vain.

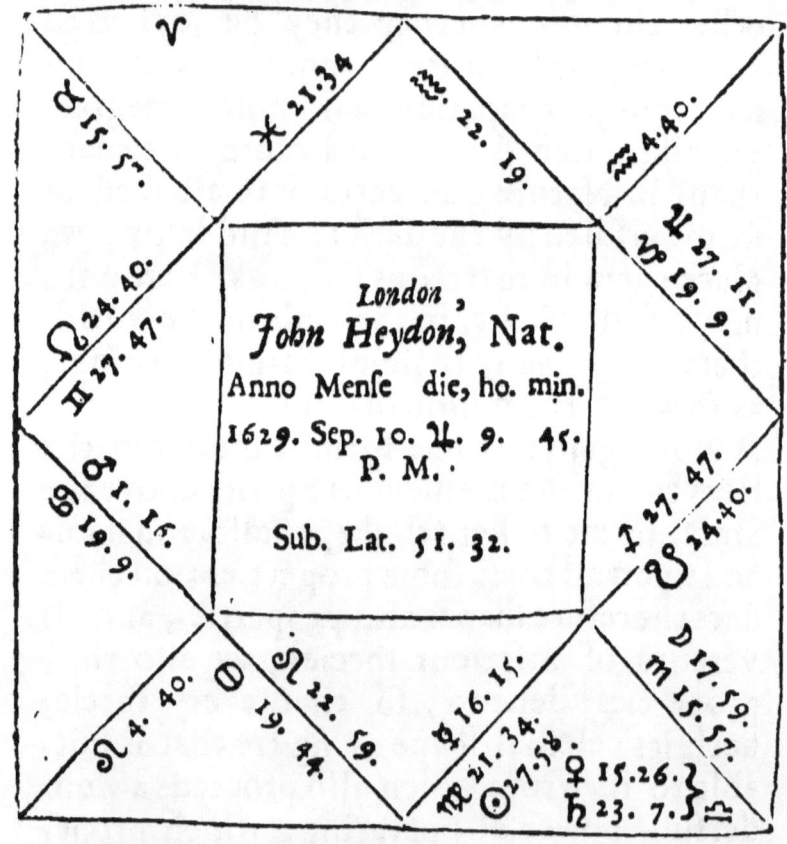

These virtues and *Genii* do not err in their

actings, but by accident, *viz.* by reason of the impurity, or inequality of the matter; for upon this account, there are found things of the same species, more or lesse powerfull, according to the purity or indisposition of the matter: For all celestial influences may be hindred by the indisposition, and insufficiency of the Matter; but I must haft the *Genii* to their Vehicles & then body them in a Terrestrial *Idea*, or a form of flesh, as followeth.

By an Example of a Figure of *Heaven*, 1629. *Sep.* 10. 45. 9h. P.M. to finde the name of my *Genius*, I look the places of the five *Hylegians*, and making projection always from the beginning of *Aries*, & the Letters being found out, and being joyned together according to the degree ascending, make the name of my Genius *Malhitiriel*, who had upon Earth familiarity with Elias, and many good spirits are wont to shew themselves, and be associates with the souls of them, that are purified; Examples of which, there are many in sacred Writ; as *Adam* had familiarity with the angel *Raziel*, *Shem* the son of *Noah* with *Jophiel*,

phiel, *Abraham* with *Zadkiel*, *Isaac* and *Jacob* with *Peliel*, *Joseph*, *Joshua* and *Daniel* with *Gabriel*, *Moses* with *Metattron*, *Elias* with *Malbitiriel*, *Tobias* the younger with *Raphael*, *David* with *Cerniel*, *Mannoah* with *Phadael*, *Job* with *Cenez*, *Plato* with *Cerrel*; *Ezekiel* with *Asmael*, *Esdras* with *Uriel*, *Solomon* with *Michael*, *Socrates* with *Levaniel*, *Gideon* with *Semiliel*, &c. And the names of *Genii* are made by *Hebrew*, *Greek*, *Chaldean*, *Arabick*, *Ægyptian* or *Latine* letters, from the degree of the Afcendent, through each degree according to the order of fignes to caft the Letters; and what letters fall into the places of the aforefaid ftars found out above, and rightly joyned together, make the name of a *Genius*; but fome curious wits have conceited, that my going to fchool in *Warwick-shire* amongft my *mothers friends* one while, and afterwards in *Devonshire* amongft my *Fathers friends*, changes the Nature of my *Genius*; they are miftaken, although I have been in *Italy*, *Spain* and *Turkey*, and many other parts of the world, yet is my *Genius* not changed; For *Mercury* my Significator in *Virgo*, and *Venus* in *Libra*, give me the Nature of my *Genius*; and *Gemini* will be my Afcendent: Here they object again, that it fals out, that men of a differing Nature and Fortune do often-
times

The Harmony of the World.

times by reason of the same Ascendent and name, obtain the same *Genius* of the same name: Note the Position of the Heavens may differ by the Planets places; *Although* Elijah *had the same I have from Heaven*; and you must know therefore, that it must not be thought absurd, that the same *Angel* may be separated from any one *soul*, and the same be set over more: And yet the *soul* after the *Death* of the *Body wears the same name* the *Priest*, *Godfathers*, *Mothers* and *Parents* consented to give the body at *Baptism*, *as guided by God the chief Father*. Now they finde out an evill *Genius* from the *Almutez* of the Angle of the Twelfth House, which they call an evill spirit, casting from the degree of the falling, against the progresse of the signes. And as divers men have many times the same name, so also spirits of divers Offices and natures may be noted or marked by one name, by one and the same *Seal* or *Character*, yet in a different respect; for as the *Serpent* doth sometimes typifie *Christ*, and sometimes the *Devill*, so the same names, and the same Numbers and Seals may be applyed sometimes to the order of a *good spirit*, and sometimes to the order of a *bad*: And as there is *A Heaven above, so there is a Heaven below; and as there are Stars above, so there are Stars*

H 3 *below*

below; and all that is above is also below, which makes the Harmony and agreement of the World. And this is the Figure of the Earth

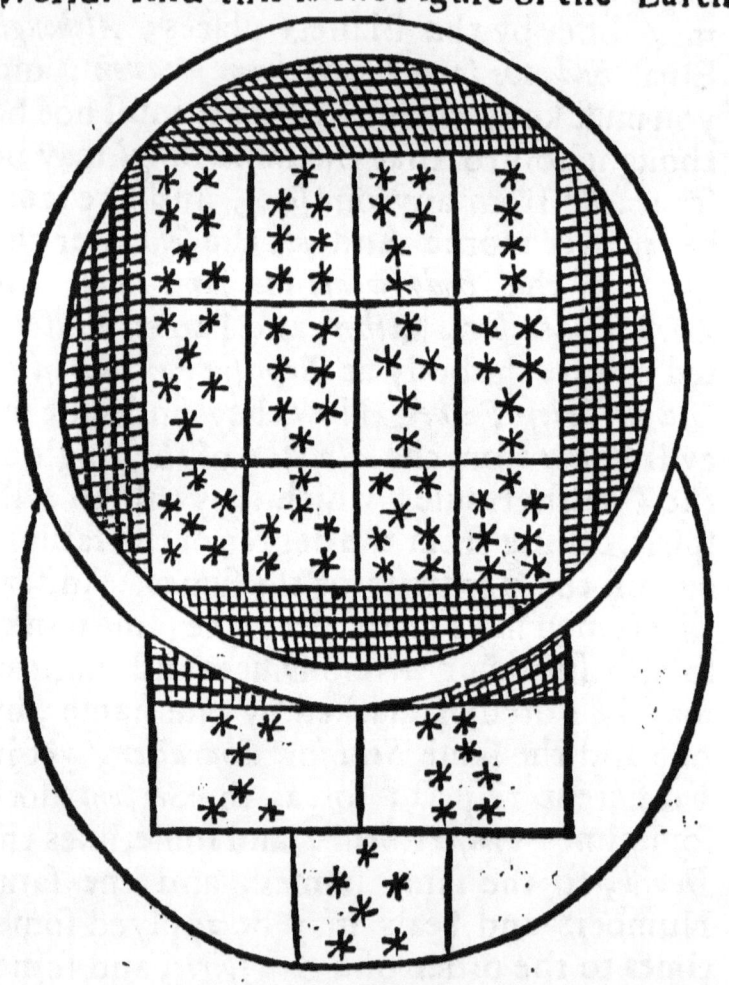

in which I was born; and as you may see in my *Rosie Crucian Infalible Axomata*, how numbers

The Harmony of the World.

numbers work upon the soul; so you may see in my three Books which were the title of *The Temple of Wisdome*, how these figures work upon the body, and *Harmony* upon the whole *Animal*; And there is *a secret divine power* in them, as there is in Herbs and Plants that Cure Diseases. Again, there are *Spirits* in the *Earth* that *vivifie* all things upon the Earth, and there is *a spirit* in the *water* that *causes the flux*, and *influx* of the *Sea*; and these are the *Characters* of the *ministring spirits*, which St. Paul saith, *were sent forth to them who shall be heires of salvation*. And we read in *Esay, The Angels of the Lord went forth, and flew in the Tent of the Assyrians One hundred eighty-five thousand;* And these *are the sons of the Oyle of splendour*, we read of in *Zachary*, who assist the *Rulers of the whole* Earth: And the highest place of these Orders below, are those which they call היותהקדש, *i. e.* creatures of Holinesse, by the which *God giveth the gift of Being*. In the second place, succeed *Ophanim*, *i. e.* forms or Wheels, by the which *God distinguisheth the Chaos*: In the third place are
Aralim

Aralim, i. e. great, strong and mighty Angels, by the which *Jehova Elohim* pronounced, or *Jehovah* joyned with *He*, *Administreth Form to the liquid Matter*: In the fourth place are *Hasmalim*, by which *El*, *God frameth the Effigies of bodies*; The fifth order is from *Seraphim*, by the which *God Elohim Giber draweth forth the Elements*; The sixth is *Malachim*, i.e. of Angels, by the which God *Elcha* produceth metrals: The seventh *Elohim* i e. the *spirits* of the *Earth*, by the which God *Jehovah Sabaoth* procreateth *Animals*: The nineth is from *Cherubim*, by the which God *Sadai* created Mankinde. The tenth *Issim*, i. e. Nobles, strong men, or blessed, by the which God *Adonai* bestoweth *Knowledge* in *Nature*, *Reason*, *Philosophy* and *Divinity*, and thus are the works of God done in *Earth*, as they are in *Heaven Harmoniously*.

Chap.

Chap. IX.

How the Genii *are united to their different Vehicles; Of* Ætherial *and* Terrestrial *Vehicles. The Duration of the* Genii *in their several Vehicles necessary for the understanding, how they enter into this Earthy body.*

For your better understanding how a *pre-existent Genius* may enter this *Terrestrial body*, there are two things to be enquired into, the diference of the *Vehicles* of *Genii*, and the cause of their union with them: The *Platonists* doe chiefly take notice of three kindes of *Vehicles, Æthereal, Aereall* and *Terrestrial*; And now I shall shew you how the *genius* is united to the body, or terrestrial Vehecle by the *medium* or spirit of the world; for there is nothing of such transcending vertues, which being destitute of divine assistance, is content with the Nature of it self.

And these divine powers, which are diffused into things are *Lights, Genii* or *Idea's* call them which you will: For the vertue of things depend upon these, because it is the property of the *Soul* to be from one matter extended into divers things; and sometimes the

the *soule* of one thing, they say goes out into another: altering it and hindering the operations of it. As the soul of fals-hearted *courſe-natured Scolds* offend the fine temper of of a *delicate ſweet natured Woman*; and the ſpirits of the firſt ſort, they ſay, goes into the *Daws* and *Crows*; but the ſecond will ſure inhabite the *Etherial Region*, the Country of God.

And the *Diamond* hinders the operation of the *Load-ſtone*, that it cannot attract Iron, now ſeeing the ſoule is the firſt that is movable, and as they ſay, is moved of it ſelf; but the body, or the matter is of it ſelf unable, and unfit for motion, and doth much degenerate from the *ſoule*, therefore there is a more excellent *medium*, *viz.* ſuch a one that may be as it were no body, but as it were a *ſoule*, or as it were no *ſoule*, but as it were a body: *viz.* by which the ſoule may be joyned to the body; now ſuch a Medium I conceive is the *ſpirit of the World*, *viz.* that which we call the *Quinteſſence*: becauſe it is not from the foure Elements, but a certaine firſt thing, having its being above, and beſides them.

There is therefore ſuch a kinde of Spirit required to be, as it were the Medium, whereby *Cæleſtiall Genii* are *Joyned to groſs bodyes of red Earth*, and beſtow upon them wonderfull

The Harmony of the World. 107

full gifts. This spirit is after the same manner in the body of the world, as a *Genius* is in the body of a man: For as the powers of our souls are communicated to the members of the body by the spirit, so also the vertue of the soul of the world is difused through all things by the Quinteſſence.

For there is nothing found in the whole world, that hath not a sparke of the vertue thereof; yet it is more, nay, moſt of all infuſed into thoſe things which have received or taken in moſt of this ſpirit, now this ſpirit is received or taken in by the *Rays* of the *Stars*, ſo farr forth as things render themſelves conformable to them; by this *spirit* every property is conveyed into *Herbs, Stones, Metals* and *Animals*, through the *Sun, Moon, Planets*, and through *Stars* higher then the *Planets*: Now this ſpirit may be more advantageous to us, if any one knew how to ſeparate it from the *Elements*; or at leaſt to uſe thoſe things chiefly, which do moſt abound with this ſpirit, for theſe things, in which this ſpirit is leſſe drowned in a body, and leſs checqued by matter, do more powerfully, and perfectly act, and alſo more readily generate their like. For in it are all generative and ſeminary vertues, for which cauſe, ſome *Doctors* and *Alchimiſts* endeavour to ſeparate this ſpirit
from

from *Gold*, and make the *Pentarva*, which is easy but very costly, but if it be rightly separated from *Gold* and *Silver*; if you shall afterwards project upon any matter of the same kinde, (*i.e.*) any mettall, will presently turn it into *Gold* or *Silver*, and I know how to do that, and have seen it done but we could make no more *Gold*, then the weight of that was, out of which we extracted the spirit. For seeing that is an extence forme, and not intence, it cannot beyond its own bounds change an imperfect body into a perfect, which I deny not but may be done by another way.

Now originally *man* was taken out of the great *World*, as woman was taken out of Man: For man was a piece of *Red earth*: But while I contemplate this strange vertue of the spirit of the world, the power of the soule of the woman comes into my minde; in which there is no such measure or exaltednesse, that it should be able to act such Miracles, as I may so call them, rather then natural effects: I cannot but be more then usually inclinable to think that the Plastick power and faculty of the soule of the Infant, or whatever accessions there may be from the imagination of the Mother, is not the adæquate cause of the Formation

of

of the *Fœtus*; but if you think this is onely my bare word, read *Orpheus, Synefius*, and *Zoroafter*: and they will be my Authority for this Doctrine.

If this be not enough, I will follow the *method of God*, & examine the nature & composition of man: You finde in *Genesis* that *God* made him out of the *Earth*; This is a great myftery, For it is not the *common Pot Clay*, but an other thing, and that of a far better nature: He that knows the subject of the *Philofophical Medicine* and the *Pantacæa*, and other secrets, how to cure all difeafes, & raife the Dead to life again, and by confequence know what deftroys or preferves the temperament of man: And in man are three principles homogenial with his life, such as can reftore his decayes, and reduce his diforders to a *Harmony*. They that are ignorant in this point are not competent *Judges* of *life* and *Death*, but *Quacks* and *Pifpots Doctors*.

To unite the foule to the body, the spirit of Nature affifts this performance; so we have difcovered a caufe proportional to so prodigious an Effect: For we may eafily conceive that the deeply impaffionated fancy of the Mother fnatches away the *spirit of Nature* into *Confent*, which spirit may rationally be acknowledged to have a hand in the efformation

mation of all vitall Beings in the world, and haply be the onely Agent in forming of all manner of Plants.

In which kinde, whether she exert her power in any other *Elements* then *Earth* and *Water*: I will conclude no further than that there may be a possibility thereof in the calmer Regions of *Aire* and *Æther*; To the right understanding of which conjecture, some light will offer it self, from what I have said, concerning the visibility and consistency of the *Aerial Dæmons*, in their occursions one from another.

But this is not the onely Argument that would move one to think that this *Spirit of Nature* intermeddles with the Efformation of the *Fætus*; for those signatures, *viz. marks, moles* and *Scars*, that are derived from the *Mothers fancy*, in the Act of Conception, cannot well be understood without this *Hypothesis*; For what can be the subject of that Signature? Not the Plastick part of the soul of the Mother.

For that, it is not the Mothers soule that efforms the *Embrio* (as *Epicharmus, Cebes, Psellus* and *Proclus*, ingeniously conjecture, from the manner of the Efformation of *Birds*, which is in their *Eggs*, distinct from the *Hen*, and they may aswel be Hatched without any Hen

Hen at all; a thing I have ordinarily seen both in *Ægypt* and *Arabia*: I have seen it also in *Italy* and in *Barbary*:) Now the *Embrio*, for it hath yet no body, nor its *Genius*, for the *Soule*; if we believe *Plato* and *Boethius*, is not yet present there. But the *Spirit of Nature* or *mediũ* is present every where, which is *snatcht* into consent by the force of the Imagination of the Mother, retains the Note, and will be sure to seale it on the body of the Infant.

For what rude inchoations the soul of the world has begun in the Matter of the *Fætus*, this signature is comprehended in the whole designe; and after compleated by the presence and operation of the Particular *soule* of the *Infant*, which co-operates conformably to the Pattern of the *Soule of the world*, and insists in her footsteps, who having once begun any hint to an entire designe; she is alike able to pursue it in any place, she being every were like, or rather the same in her self: For as our *Genius*, being one, yet, upon the various temper of the *Spirits*, exerts her self into various imaginations and conceptions; so the *Genius* of the world, being the same perfectly every where is engaged to exert efformative power every where alike, where the matter is exactly the same.

Whence

Whence it had been no wonder, if those *Chickens* above mentioned, sometimes marked with *Hawkes heads*, had been hatched an hundred miles distant from the Hen, whose imagination was disturbed in the act of conception; because the *soul of the world* had begun a rude draught, which it self would as necessarily pursue every where; This opinion therefore of *Plato* is neither irrational nor unintelligible, That the *Anima Mundi* interposes and insinuates into all Generations of things, while the matter is fluid and yeilding, which would induce a man to believe, that she may not stand idle in the transfiguration of the *Vehicles* of the *Genii*, but assist their fancies and desires; and so help to cloath them, and attire them according to their own pleasures; or it may be sometimes against their wills, as the unweildinesse of the Mothers fancy forces upon her a monstrous birth.

Now the soul faln into this low and fatall condition, where she must submit to the course of Nature, and the laws of other Animals, that are generated here on Earth, displayes her self by degrees, from smaller dimensions to the Ordinary size of men, when as this faculty of contracting and dilating of

The Harmony of the World.

of themselves is in the very essence and *Idea* of all *Spirits*; as I have written in my second book *of the Rosie Crucian Physick*, cap. 3. So she does but that leasurely and naturally now, being subjected to the laws of this *Terestrial Fate*, (as I have noted in *the Idea of the Law*) which she does, exempt from this condition suddenly and freely : Not growing by *juxta* —— position of parts, or intromission of matter; but inlarging of her self with the body, meerly by the *Dilatation* of her own Substance, which is one and the same alwayes. And now I shall speak of the Harmony of mans body, how the soul fashions it.

Chap.

Chap. X.

Of the Harmony *of the* Microcosme, *how the Spirit or* Genius *proportions the body: How the* Body *agrees with* Musick, *and of the measure and Number of Members in Man.*

MAn in his *Original* was a branch planted in God, and behold he is the most beautifull and perfectest of his works, wearing his Image yet, and is called the lesser world; Therefore he by a more perfect composition and sweet *Harmony*, and more sublime dignity doth contain and maintain in himself all *Numbers, Measures, Weights, Motions, Elements,* and all other things which are of his Composition.

And in him, as it were, in the supream workman-ship, all things obtain a certain high condition, beyond the ordinary consonancy, which they have in other Compounds: From hence in old time, Men did Number by their Fingers, and shewed all Numbers by them: And they seem to prove that from the *very joynts of mans body,* all *Numbers, Measures, Proportions,* and *Harmonies* were *invented and contrived,*

And

The Harmony of the World.   115

And according to the Meafure of the body, is framed *Temples, Palaces, Churches, Chappels, Abbeyes. Houfes, Theaters*; alfo *Ships Guns, Engins*, and every kinde of Artifice; and all members of Edifices and buildings, as *Columns*,

lumns, Chapiters, of *Pillars, Basis, Buttresses, Feet* of *Pillars*, &c. Moreover *God* himself taught *Noah* to build the *Arke*; according to the measure of Mans body; and he made the whole Fabrick of the world proportionable to Mans body; therefore it is called the great World, mans body the lesse.

Therefore al those who have written of the Microcosme or of man, measure the body by six feet, a foot by ten degrees, every degree by five minuites; and thus we number sixty degrees, which make three hundred minuits, to the which are compared so many *Geometrical Cubits*; by which *Moses* describes the *Arke*: For as the body of man is in length three hundred minuites, in breadth fifty, in height thirty.

So the length of the *Arke* was three hundred Cubits, the breadth fifty, and the height thirty; that the proportion of the length to the breadth be six fold, to the height ten fold, and the proportion of the breadth to the height about two thirds: In like manner the Measures of the Members are proportionate, and consonant both to the parts of the world, and Measures of the *Archetype*, and so agreeing, that there is no member in man, which hath not correspondence with some signe, Star, *intelligence*, Divine name,

some-

sometimes in *God* himself, the *Archetype*; but the whole measure of the body may be turned, and proceeding from roundnesse, to turn and tend to it again: And the body may be measured many wayes; for example, If a man be placed upright, with his feet together and his Armes stretched forth, he will make a Quadrature equilateral, whose Centre is the bottome of the belly: But if on the same Centre, a Circle be made, by the Crown of the Head, the Arms being let fall so far, till the end of the Fingers touch the Circumference, make as much as the Fingers ends are distant from the top of the head.

Then they divide that Circle, which was drawn from the Centre of the lower belly, into five equall parts, which do constitute a perfect *Pentagon*; and the heels of the Feet, having reference to the Navile, make a *Triangle* of equal sides; but if the heels being unmoved, the Feet be stretched forth on both sides, to the right and left, and the hands lifted up to the line of the Head, then the ends of the Fingers and Toes do make a square of equal sides, whose centre is on the Navile; as if a man stood in the middest of a Figure, and his hands made shorter by the fourteenth part of his upright stature; then the distance of his Feet having reference to the

the lower belly, they will make an equilateral *Triangle*; and the Centre being placed in his Navile, a Circle being brought about will touch the *ends* of the Fingers and Toes. And if the hands be lifted up as high as may be, above the Head, then the Elbows will be equall to the Crown of the Head; and i then the Feet being put together, a mar stand streight, he may be put into an equilaral square brought by the extremities of the Hands and Feet.

The Centre of this square is the Navile which is the middle betwixt the top of the Head and the Knees; Observe the Compass of a Man under the Arm-pits contains the middle of his length, whose middle is the bottome of his breast, and from thence upward to the middle of his breast betwixt both duggs, and from the middle of his breast unto the crown of his head, on every side the fourth part: also from the bottome of his breast to the bottome of his knees, and from thence to the bottome of his ankles the fourth part of a man, the same is the latitude of the shoulder blades, from one extream to another, the same is the length from the elbow to the end of the lowest finger, and therefore this is called a Cubit.

Thus we count foure Cubits make the length

length of a man, and one Cubit the breadth, which is in the shoulder blade, but that which is in the compaſſe one foot; now ſix hands breaths make a Cubit, foure a foot, and foure finders breadth make a hand breadth, and the whole length of a man is twenty four hand breadths, of ſix foot, of ninty ſix fingers breadths, from the bottom of his breaſts to the top of his breaſts, is the ſixth part of his length, from the top of his breaſt to the top of his forehead and lowermoſt root of his haires, the ſeventh part of his length.

Of a ſtrong and well ſet body, a foot is the ſixth part of the length, but of a tall the ſeventh. Neither can (as *Zoroaſter*, and *Jarchas* teſtifie) the talneſſe of mans body exceed ſeven feet, the *Diameter* of his Compaſs is the ſame meaſure, as is from the hand being ſhut unto the inward bending of the elbow, and as that which is from the breaſt to both duggs, upward to the upper lip, or downward to the navel; and as that which is from the ends of the bones of the uppermoſt part of the breaſt, compaſſing the Gullet, and as that which is from the ſole of the foot to the end of the Calfe of the legg, and from thence to the middle whirle bone of the knee, all theſe meaſures are co equall,

and

and make the seventh part of the whole height.

The head of a man from the bottome of the chin to the crowne of his head, is the eighth part of his length, as also from the elbow to the end of the shoulder-blade: so great is the Diameter of the compasse of a tall man; the Compasse of the head drawn from the top of the forehead, and the bottome of the hinder part of the head, make the first part of his whole length, so much also doth the breadth of the breasts, nine face breadth make a square well set man, and ten a tall man.

The length of man therefore being divided into nine parts, the face from the top of the forehead to the bottome of the chin, is one, then from the bottome of the throat, or the top of the breast unto the top of the stomack is another, from thence to the navile is a third, from thence to the bottome of the thigh a forth, from thence the hip to the top of the calfe of the legg makes two, from thence to the joynt of the foot makes two more, all which are eight parts.

The space from the top of the forehead to the crowne of the head, and that which is from the chin to the top of the breast, and that which is from the joynt of the foot, to the

the sole of the foot, I say these three spaces joyned together make the ninth part; in breadth, the breast hath two parts, and both arms seven, but the body, which ten face breadths make, is the most exactly proportioned.

Therefore the first part of this, is from the crowne of the head to the bottome of the nose, from thence to the top of the breast, the second; and then to the top of the stomack the third; and from thence to the navile, the fourth; from thence to the privy members the fift; where is the middle of the length of man; from whence to the sole of the feet, are five other parts; which being joyned to the former, make ten whole; by which every body is measured by a proportioned measure. For the face of a man from the bottome of his chin, to the top of his forehead, and bottome of the haire is the tenth part: The hand of a man from the shutting, to the end of the longest finger is also one part; also betwixt the middle of both duggs is one part, and from both to the top of the gullet is an equilaterall triangle, the lattitude of the lower part of the forehead from one eare to the other is another part: the latitude of the whole breast,

viz.

viz. from the top of the breasts to the joynt of the shoulder blades, is on both sides one part, which make two; the compasse of the head crofs-wife from the distance of the eye-browes by the top of the forehead unto the bottome of the hinder part of the head, where the haire ends, hath also two parts; from the shoulders on the outside unto the coupling together of the joynts of the Hand, and on the inside from the Arme-pits unto the beginning of the palme of the Hand, and of the Fingers, are three parts. The compasse of the Head by the middle of the Forehead hath three parts; the compasse of the Girdling hath foure parts in a well set man, as (faith *Pomponatius*) but in a thin body three parts and a halfe, or as much as is from the top of the breast to the bottome of the Belly; the compasse of the Breast by the arm-pit to the Back hath five parts, *viz.* as much as half the whole length from the Crowne of the head to the knurles of the Gullet, is the thirteenth part of the whole altitude; the Armes being stretched upward, the Elbow is even to the Crown of the Head.

But now let us see how equall the other commensurations are to one the other, as much as the distance is from the chin to the top of the Breast, so great is the latitude of the

the Mouth, as much as is the diftance betwixt the top of the breaft, to the Navile, fo great is the compaffe of the Mouth; as much as the diftance is from theChyn to the crown of the head, fo great is the latitude of the girdling place; as is the diftance from the top of the Nofe to the bottome, fuch is the diftance betwixt the chin and the throat;Alfo the cavity of the eyes from the place betwixt the eye-browes unto the inward corners, and the extention of the bottome of the Nofe; & the diftance from the bottome of the Nofe to the end of the upper lip; I fay thefe three are equall amongft themfelves, and as much as from the top of the Nayle of the forefinger to the lowermoft joynt thereof; and from thence where the hand is joyned to the arme on the outfide, and in the infide from the top of the nayle of the middle finger unto the lowermoft joynt, and from thence to the fhutting of the hand : I fay all thefe parts are equall amongft themfelves; the greater joynt of the forefinger, equalls the height of the forehead; the other two to the top of the Nail, equall the Nofe; from the top to the bottome, the firft and the greater joynt of the middle finger equall the fpace which is betwixt the end of the Nofe

Nose to the end of the Chyn, and the second joynt of the middle finger is as much as the distance from the bottome of the Chin to the top of the lower Lip, but the third is from the mouth to the end of the Nose, but the whole hand as much as the whole face.

The greater joynt of the Thumb is as much as the widenesse of the Mouth, and as the distance betwixt the bottome of the chin and the top of the lower lip, but the lesser joynt is as much as the distance betwixt the top of the lower and the end of the nose; the Nailes are half as much as those joynts, which they call the Nayle joynts, the distance betwixt the middle of the eye-browes to the outward corners of the Eyes, is as much as betwixt those corners of the Ears; the height of the Forehead, the length of the Nose, and the widenesse of the Mouth are equall; also the breadth of the Hand and Foot are the same; the distance betwixt the lower part of the Ankle to the top of the Foot is the same, as that betwixt the top of the foot, and the end of the Nayles.

The distance from the top of the Forehead to the place bewixt the Eyes, and from that to the end of the Nose; and from thence to the end of the Chin is the same; the Eyebrows joyned together, are as much

as

as the Circle of the Eys, and the half Circle of the Ears equals the widenesse of the mouth; whence the Circles of the Eys, Ears and Mouth opened are equal; the breadth of the Nose is as much as the length of the eye;

And therefore the Eyes have two parts of that space, which is betwixt both extremities of the Eyes, a third part the Nose that is betwixt takes up: From the Crown of the Head to the Knees, the Navile is the middle; from the top of the Breast to the end of the Nose, the Knuckle of the Throat makes the middle; from the Crown of the Head to the bottome of the Chin, the Eyes are the middle; from the space betwixt the Eyes to the bottome of the Chin, the end of the Nose is the middle; from the end of the Nose to the bottome of the Chin, the end of the lower Lip is the middle, a third part of the same distance is the upper Lip: And all these Numbers, Measures and Weights are through manifold proportions and harmonical consents Consonant one to the other: For the Thumb is to the Wrist in a circle Measure in a double proportion and a half, for it contains it twice and a half, as five is to two.

But the proportion of the same to the brawn of the Arm neer the Shoulder is triple

triple, the greatneffe of the Legs is to that of the Arm, a proportion halffo much again, as of three to two. And the fame proportion is of the Neck to the Leg, as of that to the Arm, the proportion of the Thigh is triple to the Arm; the proportion of the whole body to the Trunck is eight and a half; from the Trunck or Breaft to the Legs, and from thence to the foles of the Feet, a third and a half; from the Neck to the Navile, and to the end of the Trunck a double.

The latitude of them to the latitude of the thigh is halffo much again: of the head to the Neck triple, the fame to the leg. The length of the Fore-head betwixt the Temples is fourefold to the height thereof; thefe are thofe meafures which are every where found, by which the members of mans body according to the length, breadth, height, and circumference thereof agree among't themfelves, and alfo with the celeftials themfelves: all which meafures are divided by manifold proportions, either upon them that divide, or are mixed, from whence there refults a manifold Harmony.

For a double proportion makes thrice a *Diapafon*, foure times double twice a Diapafon, and *Diapente*; after the fame manner are Elements, Qualities, Complexions; and
humours

humors proportioned. For these weights of humours and complections are assigned to a *sound and well compofed man, viz.* the three weights of blood, of flegme foure, of choller two, of melancholy one; that on both sides there be by order a double proportion; of the first to the third, and of the second to the fourth, a *foure times* double proportion: but of the first to the last an eighth fold.

Mebabel Olopuen faith, that the heart of a man in the first year hath the weight of two Drams, in the second, foure; and so proportionably in the fifty year to have the weight of an hundred Drams; from which time the decreases are again reckoned to an equilibrium; which the course being ended, may return to the same limit, and not exceed the space of life by the decay of that member, by which account, of one hundred years, he circumscribed the life of man. And *Empidocles* and *Jambicus* are of the same opinion; therefore doe I intend *Rofie Crucian Medicines* in their proper places to *prolong life, preserve health, keep people young, wife and vertuous, and change, alter and amend the state of the body* if need require it.

The Motions also of the Members of mens bodies answer to the motions of the *spirits,* that move the *Spheres* upon their *whirling Vortices,*

Vortices, turning and straining the *Planets* this way and that way, and every man hath in himself the motion of his heart, which answer to the motion of the *Sun*; and being diffused through the Arteries into the whole body, signifies to us, by a most sure rule, *Years*, *Moneths*, *Dayes*, *Houres* and *Minuits*.

There is a certain Nerve found by the *Anatomists* about the middle of the Neck-pit, which being touched, doth so move all the members of the body, that every one of them move according to its proper motion: by which like touch *Damabiah kim Cim*, thinks the members of the world are moved by God: And there are two Veins in the Neck, which being held hard, the mans strength failes immediately, and his senses are taken away untill they be loosened.

Therefore the eternal Maker of the *World*, when he was to put the Soul into the Body, and into its habitation; first made a fit lodging worthy to receive it, and endows the most excellent *Soul* with a most beautifull Body, and then the *Soul* knowing its own *Divinity*, frames and adorns for its own habitation. Thus the People of *Persia*, *Greece*, *Arabia*, *Italy*, *Spain* and *France*, which were governed by wise men, did make them *Kings*, Not of those which were most strong, wealthy,

thy, but those onely which were most *proper* and *beautifull*; for they conceived, that the *Gallantry* of the *minde*, *did depend upon the excellency of the body*, which such as searched into the secrets of Causes, hid in the very Majesty of Nature, were bold to assert, that there was no fault of, and no disproportion in the Body, which the Vice and Intemperance of the Minde did not follow; because it is certain, that they doe increase, thrive and operate by the help one of the other: And now let us see where the *Soule* or *Genius* is seated.

Chap. XI.

In what part of the body, is. the chief seat of the soul; that common sense is seated somewhere in the head, a caution for the choyce of the particular place thereof; that the whole braine is not it, nor any small solid particle, nor any externall membrane of the Braine, nor the Septem Lucidum *nor the* Conarion, *nor that part of the spinall marrow where the* Nerves *are con-*

K *ceived*

ceived to concurr, but the spirits in the fourth Ventricle of the Braine; that neither the soul without the spirits, nor the spirits without the presence of the Genius in the Organ, are sufficient causes of sensation; how sensation is made; how imagination, of reason and memory; and whether there be any markes in the braine, that the spirits are the imediate instrument of the Genius in memory also; and how memory arises, as also forgetfullness, how spontanious motion is performed; how we walke, sing, and play, though thinking of something else; that though the spirits be not alike every where, yet the sensiferous impression will pass to the common sensorium, that there is a heterogenity in the very soul her self, and what it is in her we call the root and centre, and the eye; and what the rayes and branches, that the sober and allowable distribution of her into parts, is into perceptive and plastick.

IF there be granted a *Genius* in the Body, that the Head is the chief Seat thereof, & place of common sense; & that no man hereafter may make any other unhappy choice in the parts of the Body, we shall now propose such Reasons, as we hope will plainly prove, that the common Sensorium must needs

needs be in the Head; or indeed if we prove that the Heart is not the seat of common sense, nor any smal solid particle, nor any external membrane of the Brain: Nor the *septem Lucidum*, nor the *Conarium*; it will follow according to this *Hypothesis*, that the Head is: As that out of *Cornelius Agrippa*, that a Nerve being tyed, Sense and Motion will be preserved from the Ligature upwards to the Head, but downwards they will be lost: As also that experiment of *Cardanus* by a Frog, whose Brain he peirced, and presently the Frog was devoid of sense and motion, and if you take the entrailes out, it will skip up and down, and exercise its senses as before, which is a plain evidence, that motion and sense is derived from the Head; and there is now no pretence to trace any motion into a further fountain; the Heart (from whence the Nerves were conceived to branch by Dr. *Culpeper*, and from whence certainly the Veins and Arteries doe as appears by every Anatomy) being so justly discharged from that office. To which it may suffice to add the consideration of those diseases, that seize upon all the Animal functions at once; such as are the *Lethurgie*, *Apoplexie*, *Epilepsie*, &c. the causes of which *Rosie Crucians*, finde in the Head, and accordingly

K 2

cordingly apply Remedies; but the ordinary *Doctors of Physick* being ignorant in these things, are the destruction and death of many thousands of poore people.

Which is a plain detection that the Seat of the Soule, as much as concerns the animal faculties, is chiefly in the Head, the same may be said of *Phrensie*, and *Melancholly*, and such like distempers, that *deprave a mans Imagination and Judgement*; The *Rosie Crucians* alwayes conclude something amiss within the *Cranium*; but the *Physitians* knows not where the distemper lyes, being but little skilled in *Nature* or *Rosie Crucian Medicines*.

Lastly, if it were nothing but the neare attendance of the outward senses on the *soul*, or her discerning faculty, being so fitly placed about her in the Head; this unlesse there were some considerable Argument to the contrary, should be sufficient to determine any one that is unprejudiced, to conclude that the seat of common Sense, Understanding, and command of Motion is there also.

But now the greatest difficulty will be to define in what part thereof it is to be placed; in which, unlesse we will go over boldly and carelesly to work, we are to have a regard to Mecanical congruities, and not pitch upon
any

The Harmony of the World.

any thing, that by the Advantage of this suppofal, that there is a *Soul* in man, may go for poffible: but to chufe what is moft handfome and convenient: That the whole Brain is not the feat of *common fenfe*, appears from the Wounds and Cuts, it may receive without the deftruction of that faculty; For they will not take away fenfe and motion, unleffe they peirce fo deep as to reach the *Ventricles of the Brain*, as *Riverius* obferves.

  Nor is it in *Hypocrates* his fmal folid particle; for befides, That it is not likely the Centre of perception is fo Minute, it is very incongruous to place it in a body fo perfectly folid, more hard then *Adamant* or *Iron*; but this Invention *Ariftotle* has fome where, which is a freak of his *Petulant fancy*, that has an ambition to make a *blunder and confufion of Hypocrates*, and all other *Phylofophers* and *Phyfitians, Metaphifical fpeculations*, collecting fome and burning others, making thofe that read him believe, how though the foule were nothing but matter; yet it might be incorruptible and immortal; it was not worth the while to take notice of it here in this *Hypothefis*, which we have demonftrated to be true, *viz.* That there is a *foul* or *Genius* in the body, whofe Nature is material or corporeal.

Nor are the Membranes in the Head, the common *Sensorium*; neither those that invelop the Brain (for they would be able then to see the Light, through the whole the *trepan* makes) though the party *trepann'd* winked with his eye: (To say nothing of the conveyance of the Nerves, the Organs of external sense, that carry beyond these exteriour Membranes, and therefore point to a place more inward, that must be the recipient of all their impresses) nor any internal membrane, as that which bids fairest for it, the *Septem Lucidum*, as being in the midest of the upper *Ventricle*.

But yet if the level of motion through the external senses be accurately considered, some will shoot under, and some in a distant *paralel*, so that this membrane will not be struck with all the objects of our senses: besides that it seems odd and ridiculous, that the center of perception should be either driven out so into places, or spread into hollow convexities, as it must be supposed, if we make either the externall or internall membranes of the Braine the seat of common sense, the most likely place is the *Conarion* or the concourse of the Nerves in the fourth Ventricle of the *Animal spirits* there.

Of

Of this opinion were the brothers of the *Rosie Cross*; which would not be too long to recite here. Now the Authority of these men are not rashly to be refused, neither do I finde any Arguments hitherto that are valid enough to deface it; those that are recited out of *Avenrois, Aristotle, Pomponatius,* and *Cardanius* subscribed too by those learned Authors of *Adenographia,* and the *Hydro piromagicall Art,* have not in my judgment the force to ruine it, I shall repeat them and then examine them.

The first is, that this *Glandula* is too little to be able to represent the Images of all that the soul has represented unto her: The second, That the external Nerves do not reach to the *Glandula*; and that therefore it cannot receive the impresse of sensible Objects: The third, That it is placed in a place of Excrements, which would foile the species of things: The fourth, That the species of things are perceived there, where they are carried by the Nerves; but the Nerves meet about the beginning or head of the *spinal marrow,* a more noble and ample place then the *Glandula pinealis*.

To the first, I answer, That the amplitude of that place where the Nerves meet in the *spinal Marrow* is not large enough to receive the

the diſtinct impreſſes of all the Objects the *minde* retains in *memory*: Beſides, that the other parts of the Brain may ſerve for that purpoſe, as much as any of it can; for it is the *Soul* it ſelf alone that is capable of retaining ſo diſtinct and perfect repreſentations, though it may make an occaſional uſe of ſome private marks it impreſſes in the *Brain*; which haply may be nothing at all like the things it would remember, nor of any conſiderable magnitude nor proportion to them; ſuch as we obſerve in the words *Arx* and *Atomus*, where there is no correſpondency of either likeneſſe or bigneſſe, betwixt the words and the things repreſented by them.

To the ſecond, That though there be no continuation of the Nerves to the *Conarion*, yet there is of ſpirits; which are as able to conveigh the impreſſes of Motion from external ſenſe to the *Conarion*, as the *Aire* and *Æther* the impreſſe of the *Stars* unto the Eye.

To the third, That the *Glandula* is conveniently enough placed, ſo long as the body is ſound; for no excrementitious humours will then overflow it or beſmear it; but in ſuch diſtempers wherein they doe, *Apoplexies*, *Catalepſies*, or ſuch like diſeaſes will ariſe; which

The Harmony of the World.

which we see do fall out, let the *seat* of *common sense* be where it will.

Lastly, I say, that the Nerves, when they are once got any thing far into the *Brain*, are devoyed of *Tunicles*, and be so soft and spongy, that the motion of the *Spirits* can play through them; and that therefore they may ray through the sides, and so continue their Motion to the *Conarion*, where ever their extremities may seem to tend.

But though these Arguments do not sufficiently confute the opinion, yet I am not so wedded to it, but I can think something more unexceptionable may be found out, especially it being so much to be suspected, that all animals have not the *Conarion*, (as I have said in my book *Elias Ashmole*, Esq;) made publike, by the Title of, *The way to Blisse*.) That what pleased *Agrippa* so much in this invention, is that he conceited it such a marvelous fine instrument to beat the animal spirits into such & such pores of the Brain, a thing that I cannot at all close with: For Reasons I have given you in my Book entituled, *A New Method of Rosie Crucian Physick*; besides, that stones have been found in this *Glandula*, and that it is apparent, that it is environed with a Net of Veins and Arteries, which are indications, that it is a part

assigned

assigned for some more inferiour office: But yet I would not dismiss it without faire play.

. Wherefore that opinion of *Paracelsus* may warrant the other, who places also the seat of common sense in that part of the *spinal marrow*, where the Nerves are suspected to meet, as it is more plain and simple, so it is more irrefutable, supposing that the soule's centre of perception (whereby she does not onely apprehend all the objects of the external senses, but does imagine Reason, and freely command and determine the spirits into what part of the body she pleases) could be conveniently seated in such dull pasty matter, as the Pyth of the Brain is, a thing, I must needs confesse, that pleases not me; and therefore I will also take leave of this opinion too, and adventure to pronounce, *That the chief seat of the Genius or Soule*, where she perceives all objects, where she Imagines, Reasons, and Invents, and from whence she commands all the parts of the body, is those purer *animal spirits* in the fourth Ventricle of the Brain. The proof of this is our simpathizing so sensibly with the changes of the *Aire*, which all the learned *Astrologers* take notice of (but flattering *lying William Lilly* is not in our Harmony;) for
he

he knows nothing of *Art*, *Nature*, *Reaſon*, or *Phyloſophy*, neither doth he underſtand any of my *Books*:(And therefore without a figure, you can tell, Gentlemen, how wiſe he is;) As in clear aire, the influences of the *ſpirits* of the *Planets* and *Stars* peirce our thoughts more purely, and make them more clear, but in cloudy, they come down more obſcure & dull: So Mr. *Lilly* being ignorant of this, I have ſhut him out of our noble and admirable Society of honeſt and *Methodically* learned *Gentlemen*, *Mathematitians*, *Aſtronomers* and *Aſtrologers*, not without ſome ſcorn that he ſhould come upon the wings of honour to us, by onely the commendations of *Waſher-women*, *Rag-women* and *Pedlers*, that cry him up when Truth & all Arts & Learning cry him down: And this is the man, ſhut him out of doors, go thy ways, be gone. But take thy *Aſtrologie* or *Introduction to Horaries Queſtions* and *Nativites*, that Mr. *Nich. Fiſk*, and Mr. *John Gadbury* compoſed, which is publiſhed in thy Name along with thee; it is uſeleſſe to us, and our Harmony, it is out of Tune, no wicked Goats are admitted to our pure Concord, let us follow our way, which is by the influences, which conveys Senſe, Thoughts and Paſſions, immediately to the Soule; and they are very tenuious

and

and delicate, and of a Nature very congenerous to the Aire, with which it changes so easily.

That which makes me embrace this opinion, rather then any other is this; That first, This scituation of the common *sensorium* betwixt the *Head* and the trunk of the *Body*, is most exactly convenient to receive the impresses of Objects from both, as also to impart motion to the Muscles, in both the Head and in the Body.

And that as the *heart* pumps out *blood* perpetually to supply the whole body, with nourishment, and to keep up the bulke of this *edifice* for the *Soul* to dwell in, as also from the more subtle and agile parts thereof to replenish the Brain and Nerves with *spirits*, which are the immediate instrument of the soul for sense and motion; so it is plaine likewise, that the main use of the Brain and Nerves, is to keep these subtle spirits from overspreading dissipation, and that the Brain with its Caverns is but one great round Nerve: as the Nerves with their invisible porosities are but so many smaller productions or slenderer prolongations of the Braine.

Now unlesse the very essence of the *Genius* reach from the *Common Sensorium* to the eye, there

The Harmony of the World.

there will be very great difficulty how there shouldbe so distinct a representation of any visible object, for it is very hard to conceive, that the colours will not be confounded, and the bignesse of the object diminished, and indeed that the *Image* will not be quite lost before it come to the *Genius*, if it be only in the common Sensorium, for it is plain, and experience will demonstrate, that there is a very perfect *Image* of the object in the bottome of the eye, which is made by the discussation of the lines of Motion from it, thus the line A. B. which stands in roundnesse from the object A.C. bears against that point in the bottome of the eye in B. and the line C. D.

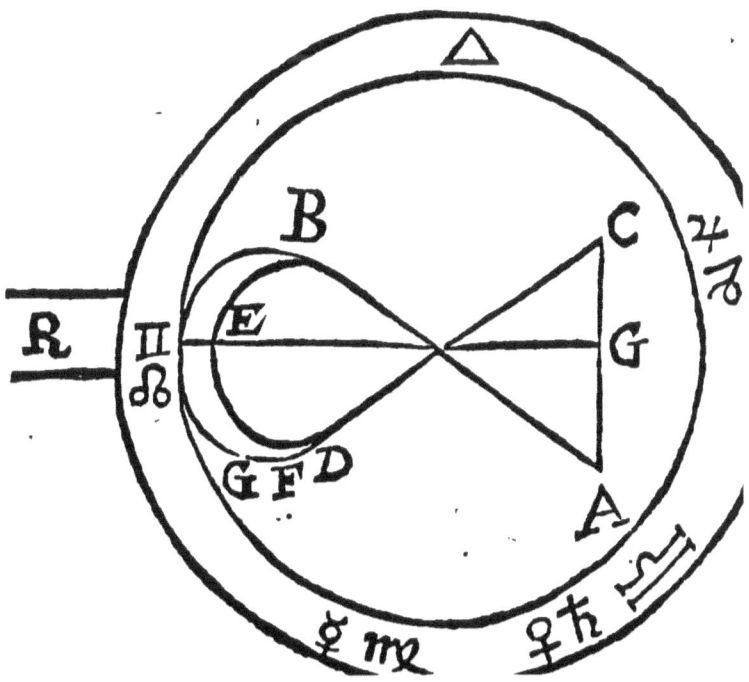

Againſt the point D. whereby C. and A. are felt in their place, and in ſuch a diſtance as they are in the objeƈt C. A. and ſo of all the lines which come from the Objeƈt C. A. into the bottome of the eye B. D. from whence the objeƈt is felt, in ſuch a length and breadth, as it is capable of being perceived in at ſuch a diſtance from the eye. And as the motion that is conveyed from A. to B. and from C. to *D.* is felt there: ſo the modification of it, whereby the objeƈts in thoſe parts may ſeem *Red, Yellow, Blew, bloome, Skeycolour, Purple, Orange, Green,* or any other colour, is felt there alſo, whence it is plaine, that there will be an exquiſite impreſſion, according to all circumſtances of the objeƈt, in the bottome of the eye; ſo that if the *Genius* receive it there, and convey it thence to her centre of perception intirely in the ſame circumſtances, the repreſentation will be compleat. But if the ſoul be not there, but the conveyance thereof muſt be left to the bare Lawes of matter, the image will be much depraved or loſt, before it can come to the Common Senſorium.

For this motion muſt be propagated from B. and D. till it come to the hole E. and ſo paſſe into the obtick Nerve, to be carried into the Brain, and ſo to the ſeat of common ſenſe:

sense: But betwixt B. and E. or D. and E. there may be the depainture of sundry colours, whence it will be necessary that F. be tinctured with the colour *D.* and *F. G.* with the Colour of both D. and F. and so of the rest of the lines drawn from the Object to the eye: so that all their colours would be blended before they come to E. Now at that harsh flexure at E. where the visuall line is as crooked as B. E. R. according to the experiments of reflection and refraction, the breadth or length of the object C. A. would be lost, for we must needs expect that, as it is in reflexions and refractions, where the object will appeare in that line, that immediately conveyes the sense of it, so here it must be also; and therefore the point C. and A. must appear about Q. whence the object will shrivel up in a manner into nothing. And suppose it might appear in some tolerable latitude, for all this the brain being an Opake substance, so soon as the motion comes thither, it would be so either changed or lost, that the image could not passe the opacity of it in any splendour of entirenesse.

 Wherefore I do not doubt but that the Image which the Genius perceives, is that in the Eye, and not any other corporeally produced

ducted to the inside of the brain (where colour and figure would be so strangely depraved, if not quite obliterated) I mean it is the concourse of the *lucid spirits*, in the bottome of the Eye, with the outward light conveyed through the humours thereof, (which is the best sense of Plato his συναύγεια wherein the great mystery of Sight consists; as you may read at large in my new Method of *Rosia Crucian* Physick.

But time passes away so hastily, that we must briefly dispatch our work : I therefore in general say, That Sensation is made by the arrival of Motion from the Object to the Organ ; where it is received in all the Circumstances we perceive it in, and conveyed by the vertue of the Souls presence there, assisted by her immediate instrument the spirits : (Now the *Genius* that enters the body, is not confined to the common *sensorium*, but does essentially reach all the Organs of the body, And by the continuity of the vertue of these Instruments to those in the common *sensorium*, the image of every object as faithfully transmitted thither.

As for imagination, there is no question, but that function is mainly exercised in the cheif seat of the soule ; those purer animal spirits in the fourth Ventricle of the *Brain*, I
speak

y of that *imagination*, which is
h as we use in erecting *Astrologi-*
d Rectifying Nativities, giving
ently upon every revolution and
projecting figures, of *Geomancy*:
e out the *Name of the Genius,*
if any one, with all the various and
encounters of this life, or such as
ie more severe *Meditations* and
Rosie Crucian Medicines, Tinctures
Iver, and all manner of *Colours*,
es, and dissolving of *Mettalls,*
dead bodies from *Death to Life* a-
ng, fresh Air, good Wine mode-
hings that tend to a handsome
puration of the spirits, make
more free, subtle and cleer.
involved together with ima-
t we need say nothing of it a-
f. Memory is a faculty of a
consideration; and if the pith
ontribute to the functions of a-
e minde (more then by concer-
nall spirits) it is to this; but
uld be stored with distinct I-
ier they consist of the flexures,
d *Fibrillæ*, or the orderly pun-
, or in a continued modifyed
ie parts thereof; some in this
L. manner

manner, and others in that) is a thing
have not only said, but proved utterly impossible: If there be any *Marks* in it, it mus[t]
be a kinde of *Trachygraphie*, some small spot
here and there standing for the recovering t[he]
memory, a series of things that would fill, i[t]
may be, many sheets of paper to write the[m]
at large.

As if a man should tye a string about [a]
friends finger to remember a businesse, tha[t]
a whole days discourse, it may be, was bu[t]
little enough to give him full instruction
in. From whence it is plain that the *Memo-*
ry is in the *Soul* and not in the *Brain*, and i[f]
she do make any such marks as we speak o[f]
she having no perception of them distin[ct]
from the representation of those thing[s]
which they are to reminde her of, she mu[st]
not make them by any *Cognitive power*, but b[y]
some such as is Analogous to her plastic
power, or faculties of Organizing the body[s]
where she acts and perceives it not.

But whether the Soul act thus or no upo[n]
the brain, is a matter of uncertain determination; nor can it be demonstrated by an[y]
experiment that I knew fit to make it intell[i-]
gible to *Lilly's Logger head*, and therefore w[e]
will containe our selves within, keeping o[ur]
lights and misteries of the Capacities of t[he]
spiri[t]

spirits to our selves, becaufe they are the immediate inftrument of the *Soul* in all her opperations, and they with the *Genius* performe all the functions of memory that we are confcious to our felves of.

And therefore I shall conclude, that memory confifts in this, that the foul has acquired a greater promptitude to think of this, or that phantafme, with the circumftances thereof, which we raifed in her upon fome occafion, which promptitude is acquired by either, the often reprefentation of the fame phantafme in her, or elfe by a more vived impreffe of it, from its Novelty, Excellency, Mifchievoufnes, or fome fuch like condition, that at once will peirce the foul with an extraordinary refentment; or finally by voluntary attention, when fhe very carefully and on fet purpofe imprints, *the Idea* as deeply as fhe can into her inward fenfe; this *promptitude* to think on fuch an *Idea* will leffen in time, and be fo quite fpent, that when the fame *Idea* is reprefented again to the foule, fhe cannot tell that ever fhe faw it before, but before this inclination thereto be quite gone, upon this pronefs to returne into the fame conception, with the circumftances; the relative fenfe of having feen it before (which we call Memory) does neceffarily emerge upon a frefh reprefentation of the Object.

But forgetfulnesse arises either out of meer desuetude of thinking on such an Object, or on others that are linked in with it, in such a series as would represent it as past, and so make it a proper Object of memory; or else for that the spirits, which the soul uses in all her Functions, be not in a due temper; which may arise from over much coolnesse, or waterishnesse in the Head, to which alone *Hypocrates* ascribes obliviousnesse.

The last thing I am to consider is *spontaneous motion*, which that it is performed by the continuation of the *spirits* from the seat of common sense to the Muscles, which is the grosse engine of Motion, is out of doubt, the manner how it is, we partly feel and see (*i e.*) We finde in our selves a power, at our own pleasure, to move this, or the other member, with very great force; and that the Muscle swels, that moves the part, which is a plain indication of influx of spirits, thither directed or there guided by our meer will; a thing admirable to consider, and worth our most serious meditation, that this direction of the Impresse of Motion, is made by our meer Will and Imagination of doing so; we know and feel it so intimately, that we can be of nothing more sure, that there is some fluid and subtile Matter, which ordinarily we we call spirits, directed into the Muscle that moves the Member, its swelling dos evidence to our sight; as also the experience that moderate use of good Wine, which supplies Spirits, will make this Motion the more strong: As for the manner, whether there be any such valvalæ or no in the Nerve, common to the opposite Muscles, as also in those that are proper to each, it is not materiall; this great priviledge of our *Souls* directing the Motion of matter thus. is wonderfull enough in either *Hypothesis:* but I look upon the *Fibrous* parts of the muscle, as the maine engine of motion; which the *soul* moistning with that subtle liquor of the *animal spirits,* makes them swell and shrinke, like *Lute strings in rainy weather.*

And in this chiefly consists, the notable strength of our Limbs in *Spontanious motion,* but for those conceived *Valvalæ,* that experience has not found out yet, nor sufficient reason, they are to wait for admission till they bring better evidence. For the presence of the animall spirits in this fibrous flesh, and the command of the soul to move, is sufficient to salve all *Phænomena* of this kinde, for upon the *will*, conceived in the *common sensorium*, that part of the *Soul* that resides in the Muscles, by a power neer a kin to that, by which she made the body, and the Organs thereof, guides the spirits into such pores and parts, as is most requisite for the shewing the use of this excellent Fabrick.

And in vertue of some such power as this, doe we so easily walk, though we think not of it, as also breath, and sing, and play on the *Lute*, *Gittarre* or *Amphorion*, though our mindes be taken up with something else; for custome is another Nature; and though the animal Spirits, as being meerly Corporeal, cannot be capable of any habits; yet the soule, even that part thereof, that is not cognitive may, and therefore may move the body, though cogitation cease, provided the members be well replenished with spirits, whose assistance in natural motions of Animals is so great, that their Heads being taken off, their Body for a long time will move as before: As *Domitian* observes in the Flies he catched and insulted over, which after he had executed his justice upon, would flye about, and use their Wings, a good part of an houre after they had lost their heads: which is to be imputed to the residence of their soule in them still, and the intirenesse of the *animal Spirits*, not easily evapourating through their craftarious Bodies, For it is but a vulgar conceit to think, that the head being taken off, the soul must presently fly out, like a Bird out of a Basket, when the lid is lifted up.

For the whole world is as much thronged up with body as where she is; and that tye of the spirits, as yet not being lost, it is a greater engagement to her to be there than any where else. This motion therefore in the Flyes about *July*, that is so perfect and durable, I hold to be vitall; but that in the parts of dismembred Creatures, that are lesse perfect, may be usually mechanical.

I have now so far forth, as it is requisite for my designe considered, the Nature and Functions of the *Soul*; and have plainly demonstrated, that she is a substance distinct from the Body, and that her very essence is spread throughout all the Organs thereof: As also that the general instrument of all her operations is the subtile spirits; which though they be not in like quantity & sincerity every where, yet they make al the body so pervious to the impresses of objects, that like lightning, they passe to the common *sensorium*: For it is not necessary that the *medium* be so fine and tenuious, as the matter where the most subtle motion begins, whence *light passe* through *Aire* and *Water*, though *Aire* alone is not sufficient for such a motion as *Light*, and

and *Water* almost uncapable of being the seat of the fountain thereof. This may serve to illustrate the passages of sense from the membranes (or in what other seat soever the *Spirits* are most subtile and *lucid*) through thicker places of the body to the very centre of perception.

And thus have I discovered a kinde of Heterogeneity in the *Soul*; and that she is not of the same power every where: For her centre of perception is confined to the fourth Ventricle of the Brain: And if the sensiferous motions we speak of be not faithfully conducted thither, we have no knowledge of the Object. That part therefore of the soul is to be looked upon, as most precious; and she not being an independent mass as matter is, but one part resulting from another; that which is the noblest is in all reason to be deemed the cause of the Rest. For which reason (as *Alfid* cals God, on whom all things depend, ῥιζῶν ῥίζαν) so, I think this part may be called the *Root of the soule*, which apprehension of our will seem the less strange, if we consider that from the highest Life, *viz. The Trinity in Unity, and Unity in Trinity*: There does result that which hath no life nor sense at all, *viz.* the stupid Matter, wherefore in very good Analogy, we may admit, mic, that that precious part of the *Soul* in which resides perception, sense, and understanding, may send forth such an essential emanation from it self, as is utterly devoid of all sense and perception, which you may call, if you will, the *exteriour branches of the Soul*, or the *Rayes or Beams of the Soul*; if you call that nobler and diviner part the *Centre*, which may very well merit also the Appellation of the Eye of the *Soul*; all the rest of its parts being but meer darknesse without it; In which, like another *Cyclops*, it will resemble the World we live in, whose one Eye is conspicuous to all that behold the light.

Now next let us prescribe Medicines Chimical, or *Rosia Crucian*, wholesome and fit to keep the Body in health and lustinesse, untill the appointed time of Death, that is, when the Soul separates from it; but we will keep them together in good temper a while with these Medicines; and then after we shall teach you the Harmony and Composition of the Humane Soule; and then conduct it to the place from whence it came.

Chap. XII.

Medicines to prolong life; to preserve health; to wax young being old; *To continue young: How to change, alter and amend the state of the Body. Of* Aurum Potabile; *Of the* Panacea; *Of the* Æther; *Of the* Pantarva: *The Water of the Sun; The Water of the Moon; The Blew Tincture and the Fire; The Greene salt and Azure Oyle; Of the red Medicine; Of the Water of the colour of Gold; Of the Oyle of Gold: How to dissolve Mettals.*

IT will not be amisse to speak something in this place of the Nature and Constitution of Man, and prescribe some Medicines that may keep the Soul and body together compleat One Hundred Years; to make that more plain which already hath been spoken.

As the *great World* consists of three parts, the *Elemental*, the *Cælestial*, and the *Spiritual*; above all which God *himself is seated in that infinite, inaccessible Light, which streames from his own Nature;* even so Man hath in him his Earthly Elemental parts, together with the Cœlestial and *Angelical Natures*, in the centre

tre of all which moves and shines the *Divine Spirit*. The Senſual, *Cœleſtial*, *Ætherial* part of man, is that whereby we do Move, See, Feel, Taſte and Smel; and have a commerce with all material objects whatſoever: It is the ſame in us as in Beaſts, and it is derived from *Heaven*, where it is predominant, to all the inferiour *Earthy* Creatures.

In plain terms, it is part of *Anima Mundi*, commonly called *Anima Media*; becauſe the influences of the *Divine Nature* are conveyed through it to the more material parts of the Creature, with which of themſelves they have no proportion. By means of this *Anima Media*, or the *Ætherial Nature*, man is made ſubject to the influence of the Stars, and is diſpoſed of *by the Cœleſtial Harmony*: For this middle ſpirit (middle I mean between both extreams, and not that which actually unites the whole together) as well that which is in the outward *heaven*, as that which is in *Man*, is of a fruitfull inſinuating nature, and carried with a ſtrong deſire to multiply it ſelf: ſo that the *Cœleſtial form* ſtirs up, and excites the *Elemental*; for this ſpirit is in *Man*, in *Beaſts*, in *Vegetables*, in *Minerals*, and in every thing, it is the Mediate of Compoſition and Multiplication.

And

And now I step from the *first Harmonicall Unity* to the *Serretum Tenebrarum*; for here I see the Creature prevaricates; you must therefore draw the *water* of the *Sun*, and the *water* of the *Moon*, for in them is *Filius solis*, and *Filia Lunæ Cœlestis*, and what offices soever the two great Lunaries perform for the conservation of the great world in general: These two little Luminaries perform the like for the conservation of their smal Cask or Microcosme in particular. And the first Medicine I shall give you the Receipt of, it will Cure all Diseases in the Body, prolong Life, Health, Youth, Wisdome, Virtue, and will alter, change and amend the state of the Body

Recep. *Limi Cœlestis partes Decem. Separatur Masculus à Fœmina, uterque porro à Terrâ suâ, phisicè tamen & citra omnem violentiam Separata proportione debitâ harmonicâ, & vitali conjungestatimque, Anima descendentia sphærâ pyroplastica, mortuum suum & relictum Corpus amplexu mirifico restaurabit conjuncta foveantur. Igne naturali in perfectum Matrimonium spiritus, & Corporis : procedas Artificio vulcanico-magico, quousque exaltentur in Quintam Rotam Metaphysicham. Hæc est, illa, de Qua tot scribillarunt tam pauci noverunt, Medicina.*

Now

Now the *Rosie Crucians*, who without controversie are the wisest of Nations, when they discourse of the generation of Mettals, tell us, it is performed in this manner. The *Mercury* or *Mineral liquor* (say they) is altogether cold and passive, and it lies in certaine earthly subterraneous caverns, but when the *Sun* ascends in the East, his beams and heat falling on this *Hemisphere*, stirr up and fortifie the inward heat of the *Earth*; thus we see in Winter weather that the outward heat of the *Sun* excites the inward naturall warmth of our bodies, and cherisheth the blood when it is almost cold and frozen.

Now then the centrall heat of the *Earth*, being stirr'd and seconded by the circumferentiall heat of the *Sun*, workes upon the *Mercury* and sublimes it in a thin vapour, to the top of its Cell or Caverne; but towards *Night* when the *Sun* sets in the *West*, the heat of the *Earth*, because of the absence of that great *Luminary* grows weak, and the cold prevailes, so that the vapours of the *Mercury* which were formerly sublimed, are now condensed, and distill in drops to the bottome of their Caverne; but the night being spent, the *Sun* againe comes about to the East, and sublimes the moisture, as formerly this sublimation

mation and condenfation continue fo long, till the Mercury takes up the *Subtle Sulphureous parts of the* Earth, and is incorporated therewith; fo that this fulphur coagulates the *Mercury*, and fixeth him at laft, that he will not fublime, but lyes ftill in a ponderous lumpe, and is concocted to a perfect mettall; our Mercury therefore cannot be coagulated without our fulphur: For it is water that diffolves and putrifies Earth, and Earth that thickens and putrifies water; you muft therefore take the *Corafcen Dog*, and the *Bitch of Armenia*, cuple them both together, and they will bring you a *skie coloured Whelp*, that will preferve health, &c. For out of the two firft principles is produced a third Agent.

But the Earth being the fubfidence or remains of that Primitive mafs, which God formed out of Darkneffe, is therefore a fæculent impure body: For the extractions which the *Divine Spirit* made were pure, *Oleous, Ætheral fubftances*, but the Crude, Phegmatick, Indigefted Humours fettled like lees towards the Centre; the Earth is fpongie, Porous and Magnetical, of compofition loofe, the better to take in the feveral Influences of Heat, Rains and Dews, for the nurture and confervation of her Products. In her is that
principal

principal refidence of that Matrix, which attracts and receives the Sperm from the Mafculine part of the world; fhe is Natures Ætna: Here *Vulcan* doth exercife himfelf, he is a pure *Cœleſtial Plaſtick Fire*, we have *Aſtrologie*, *Aſtronomy* and *Geomancy* under our Feet; the *Stars* are refident with us, and abundance of *Jewels* and *Pantarva's*, *Blew tinctures*, *Waters of the Sun and Moon*, all manner of *coloured Medicines* and *Salts*, and the green *Panacea*, the *Blew Fire*, and *Golden Water*, the *Azure Tincture*, fhe is the Nurfe and Receptacle of all things, for the fuperiour Natures ingulph themfelves into her; what fhe receives this age, fhe difcovers the next, and like a faithfull Treafurer conceals no part of her accounts.

The water hath feveral complexions according to the feveral parts of the Creature. Here below and in the circumference of all things it is volatill, crude and raw; for this very caufe, Nature makes it no part of her provifion, but fhe rectifies it firſt, exhaling it up with her heat, and then condenfing it to Rains and Dews, in which ſtate fhe makes ufe of it for nourifhment: Somewhere it is interiour, vitall and cœleſtial, expofed to the breath of the firſt Agent, and ftirred with fpiritual, eternal windes. This is that *Pſyche*

of

of *Apulejus*, and the fire of Nature is her *Cupid*; In the *Water* are hidden treasures, but so inchanted you cannot see them, for all the chest is *transparent*. I doe now advice those Gentlemen that Read me, to study Water, that they may know the Fire.

Now Nature hath for every Seed a Vessel of her own, and all her Vessels are but severall sorts of Earth, &c. The *Aurum Potabile* is so admirable a Medicine, that it cures the diseased very strangly, for they are healed unawares; Neither do they feel any operation; but suddenly they will be found & in health; there are several wayes to use this *secret virtue of Gold*, both first and last, and some of them may be communicated, but some not.

Furthermore to Cure and keep the body in health, take these approved Medicines, to nourish and fortifie your Spirits with, that which is proper to your particular infirmity, viz. The *Pantarva*, a universall Medicine, for some Temperatures; *Filius, Solis, Cælestis, Amicus Vitæ*, Proper for Surfets and cold Agues, for Lethargyes and dulnesse of Sight, *Recep Ignis Vitæ* and *Sanguis Vitæ*, for Distempers of Stomack and Bowels, in extreame swoonings; *Stella Vitæ*, in all new distempers of Bowels or Belly, Coughs, shortnesse of Breath

Breath, paſſions of the Heart, *Radix Vitæ;* the *Aurum Potabile* is well experienced to be wonderfull helpfull to women in travell, by many thouſands of people, &c. the *Aqua Solis* and *Aqua Lunæ,* cure mad people, the Spirit of *Oranges* mixed with *Deliciæ Vitæ,* cures Sadneſſe and Melancholly; Spirit of *Cinamon, Lemons* mixed with *Salus Vitæ* are good in caſes of Infectious peſtilentiall dangers, Spirit of *Angelica, Cloves* and *Roſemary* mixed, cure the Rickets, Worms, Green-ſickneſſe, Mother-fits; Spirit of *Bawme, Saffron, Mint,* and *Medulla Vitæ,* for waſtings and weakneſs; Spirit of *Clary* and *Nutmeggs,* the *Panacea* and *Succus Vitæ,* cures the Convulſion, Palſy and Falling-ſickneſſe, &c. *Spiritus Mellis* and *Luna Potabile,* cure the Dropſie, Leproſie Gout, Scurvey, Spleen, Wind, Gravell: *Adjutrix Vitæ,* cures all diſtempers of the Stomack and Bowels, and cauſeth appetite and diſgeſture: But there are many counterfeit Waters ſold by theſe names, and falſe Medicines made by thoſe who underſtand not naturall things, nor their generation, and theſe fill frail bodies full of filthy diſeaſes: To begin then to learn how to make the true medicines that will innoxiouſly and faithfully cure all diſeaſes incident to bodyes,

M you

you are to know in the first place that generation is twofold,

$\left\{\begin{array}{l}\text{Ordinary,}\\\text{and}\\\text{Extraordinary.}\end{array}\right.$

Extraordinary generation is that, by which an unlike thing is generated out of an unlike; as Mice are generated out of dung, and Snakes by putrefaction by the Sun; this Generation is termed in the Schools, *Equivocall*.

The ordinary is that, by which a like thing begets his like, as when a man begets a man child, and a Lyon a Lyon; this in the Schools is termed *univocall*, this generation with the method and the means of it; I shall include briefly thus, every thing generated or begotten, is generated and borne of his own specific seed, and in his proper Matrix.

Before any perfect thing can be generated, the seed must necessarily putrifie, and then be nourished.

The seed then putrifies, when a salt of the same nature with it, dissolved in a convenient liquor, doth by the assistance of a gentle heat penetrate, analize and rarifie the substance of the seed, that the included spirit may out of its subject matter, form a convenient

nient habitation or body for it felf; in which it may perform the Offices of natural Propagation and feminal Multiplication.

The Humour or liquor which ferves for putrefaction muft be proportionable to that body which is to be putrified; the heat which promotes this putrefaction, muft be fo milde and temperate, that the liquor in which the refolving Salt lyeth, may remain ftill in and about the matter, and not be laved or evaporated from it; the body putrifying, muft not be removed out of that Matrix, in which the putrifaction was begun, untill that which is intended be fully perfected; the more pure the Matrix is, the thing generated is by fo much the more perfect and found; that Matrix is onely convenient and adapted to Generation, which permits an eafie entrance to the feed.

Our *Salt-peter* is a moft white incombuftable body, and a gummie Aereal Nature; it is fo unctuous and aireal, it will not generate nor mingle with our due: I have for triall taken it into its groffe, and putting it in a quart of Rain diftilled: I digefted thefe two without any other third thing, for a full fortnights time; but they would never mix, the Nitre (notwithftanding many long and violent agitations of the Glaffe) keeping ftill a part a part, in the form of Butter or Oyle; more white then Snow: It is indeed of wonderfull vertue alone, &c. Bodies or substances which are generated of Ayre, retain the first complexion of their Parent: Yet I have seen Water turned into a blood'red colour, without any other thing; and I know how to do it, but I may not teach these things: Now out of that body which is either corrupted or destroyed by strange or extracious natures; or whose spermatick Vessels, are by some violence maimed or cut off, no seed can be had: That body which is preserved or sustained by one simple kinde of Nutriment; is far more perfect and durable, and yeelds more sound and prolifick seed, than that which is nourished with many and different kindes of Nutriment; by these Rules you may know how to digest, to dissolve, to putrifie, to generate, to separate the impure from the pure, and so to come by most perfect Medicines; but you must follow the method of my *Rosie Crucian* Physick, *lib.* 2. *chap* 10. you know not all nature doth. And verily, so great & precious a blessing these are, that God never imparts them to any fraudulent Montebanks, nor to Tyrants, nor to any impure lascivious Persons, nor to the

Effeminate

The Harmony of the World.

Effeminate and Idle, nor to Gluttons, nor Usurers, nor to any worshippers of *Mammon*; but in all Ages, the Pious, the Charitable, the Liberal, the Meek, the Patient and Indefatigable Spirit, who was a diligent observer and admirer of his marvelous works found out: For,

The greedy Cheat with impure hands may not,
Attempt these Arts, nor are they ever got
By the unlearn'd and rude; The Vicious minde
To lust and softnesse given, it strikes stark blinde;
So the slie wandring Factour, &c.

And again.

But the Sage, Pious man, who still adores,
And loves his Maker, and his love implores,
Who ever joyes to search the secret cause,
And series of his works, their love and laws,
Let him draw neer, and joyning will with strength
Study this Art in all her depth and length:
Then grave experience shall his Comfort be,
Skill'd in large Nature's inmost mystery;
The knots and doubts his busie course and cares
Will oft disturbe, till time the truth declares
And stable patience (through all tryals past)
Brings the glad end, and long hop'd for at last.

Behold

Behold all you Medicasters, who hate and persecute these Divine sciences *Astrology, Geomancy*, and *Chymistry*, give ear O you *Doctors* that darken counsel by words without knowledge; gird up your loyns like men, for I will demand of you, and answer you me; With what confidence can you professe your selves to be Physitians, seeing that all Physick or Medicines are without *Astrologie, Geomancy* and *Chimistry* imperfect? By the first of these we understand, from whence the disease came, and what Medicine is proper for the Patient at certain times? To Cure him according to his Temperature, which we finde by the second, and how long the sicknesse will continue? And the third supplies us out of the light of Nature, with convenient means, (and particular Natures to separate the impure from the pure) and will teach you by the first how to heale all *Diseases* of the *Macrocosmical* substances, and afterwards by examples and experiments deduced from those exteriour Cures, will shew us the right and infallible Cure of all Diseases in our own bodies? He that knows not how to heal and purge Mettals? How can he restore the decayed or weakened radical Balsome in Man? and excite it by comfortable and concordant medicines to perform per-
fectly

fectly all his appointed Functions, which must necessarily be put into action, before any disease can be expelled? He that knows not what it is in Antimony which purgeth Gold, how can he come by an effectual and wholesome Medicine, that will purge and cast out these extrarious peccant causes, and humours that afflict and destroy the body of man? He that knows not how to fix *Arsenick*, to take away the corrosive nature of *sublimate*, to coagulate *Sulphurous* spirits, and by a convenient specifical medium to break and analize stones in the greater world, will never in the body of man allay and tame the Arsenicall spirits of the Microcosmic salt; nor take quite away the venemous indisposition of the Sulphur, nor dissolve the Stone in the Bladder, and drive it out being dissolved? It is a noble, safe and pious course, to examine and try the force and virtue of Medicines upon the *Macrocosmical* substances, before we apply them to our fellow Creatures, and the rare Fabrick of Man: And yet there is none of these medicines but is so easie and cheap to be made, that a fine Chymical Lady in the making Sack-possets and Sugar-sops may practise them, and read advice to a *Daughter*, without disturbing her fancy.

The

The *Skie coloured Water*, is that in which the Azure tincture is extreamly predominant, but with much light and brightness this strange liquor, if the Sun shine on it at Noon, will attract the beams or splendor to it self, in which they will sinke downwards, as if Coagulated with the heat, but reflecteth to the eyes of the beholders, a most beautifull Rain-bow.

Take the *Ayre* of the *Fire* of our litle invisible World. For being prepared, it produceth noble effects, *Youth, Wisdome,* and *Vertue,* it will *raise the dead*, and wheresoever it appears, it is an infallible signe of life, as you see in the Spring time, when all things are green, the sight of it is cheerfull, and refreshing, beyond all imagination, it comes out of the *Heavenly earth*, for the saphir doth spermatize, and injects her tinctures into the *Æther*, where they are caried and manifested to the eye. This *Saphir* is equall of her self to the whole compound, for she is threefold, or hath in her three severall essences:

The Stone *Synochitis* brings the bearer acquainted with *Angels* and *Spirits*, the Stone *Anachitis* makes the *Images of the gods appear*, the *Ennectis* put under them, that Dream causeth *Oracles*; there is a certain vertue in
the

the *Loadstone*, by which it attracts *Iron*; *Rhubarb* expels Choller; the Oyle of that stinking loathsome weed *Tobacco* cures all manner of Wounds, but the smoak of it, is worse than any thing in the world: The *Rosie Crucians* have invented *universal Magnetic medicines* for Feavers, which being put into the Urine of a sick Patient, the quantity of a few drops will sympathetically work the same operation in the Cure of the Feaver, as the weapon Salve does upon the wound.

And there are *Medicines* with which men *may prolong their lives for ever*, they say, *raise dead Bodies to life again*; but it is not lawfull to speak and teach these things to any man: Because, whereas he has but a short time to live, yet he studies mischief with all his might, and attempt all manner of wickednesse: If he should be sure of a very long life, he would not spare God himself.

Were it not good, that we needed not to care, nor fear Hunger, Poverty, Sicknesse and Age, & that we could alwayes live so, as if we lived had from the beginning of the world; and moreover, as we should still live to the end thereof; And dwell in one place, that neither the people which dwell beyond the *River Ganges* in the Indies could hide any
thing

thing, nor those which live in *Peru* might be able to keep secret their Counsels from you.

What think you of one only Book in which you may Read, Understand and Remember, all that, which in all other Books, (which heretofore have been, and are now, and hereafter shall come out) hath been, is, and shall be learned and found out of them? How pleasant were it, if we could so sing, that instead of stony Rocks, we could draw to us Pearls and precious Stones? instead of wilde Beasts, Angels and Genii; and instead of hellish *Pluto*, move the mighty Princes of the world: *I could tell you more, for I have known some Sciences*, which you *have never heard of, nor your Fathers before you*; but I am drawing off the stage in all hast, and returning to my first solitudes, my discourse shall be therefore very short, and like the Echo's last syllables, imperfect, I intend it onely for a hint, not a full light, but a glance, and you must improve it for your better satisfaction.

Chap.

Chap. XIII.

How the Soul or Genius being united to the body continues in Harmony with it: A Comparison betwixt the Soule in the Body, and the Aerial Genii.

LEt us now convey the Soul to the place from whence it came; for all is vanity under the Sun, therefore we must first seek the Kingdome of God, &c.

O God, my life! whose *Essence* man
Is no way fit to *know*, or *scan*;
But should approach thy *Court* a *Guest*
In *thoughts* more *low*, than his *request*.
When I consider, how I stray
Me thinks 'tis pride in me to pray,
How dare I speak to *Heaven*, not fear
In all my sins to court thy *Eare*,
But as I look on *Woonts* that lurke
In blinde *Intrenchments*, and there work
Their own dark *Prisons* to repaire,
Heaving the *Earth* to take in *Aire*:
So view my fettered *Soul*, that must
Struggle with this her *load* of *Dust*

Meet

Meet her *Addresse*, and add one *Ray*,
To this mew'd *parcell* of thy *Day*
Shee would though here *imprisoned*, see
Through all her *Dirt* thy *Throne* and *Thee*,
Lord guide her out of this *sad night*
And say once more, *Let there be Light*.

 Having thus discovered the *Primitive supernatural part of the Creation*, how the *Spirits* and *Angels* descend into the *Sphers*, and give *life, light and influence* to the *Planets*, and their descent of darting of *Genii* to *man, beast* and every *living Creature*; The *Harmony of the Heavens*, *and the Harmony of mans body*: I should be in a readinesse to treat of the souls separation from it, did I not think my self obliged first to speak of the *Harmony of the Soul*; For as the *Harmony* of the *body* consists of a due measure and proportion of the members; so the Consonancy of the minde of a due temperament, and proportion of its Vertues and Operations which are *Concupiscible*, *Irascible* and *Reason*, which are so proportioned together.

 For Reason to Concupiscence hath the proportion *Diapason*, but to Anger *Diatessaron*; and Irascible to Concupiscible hath the proportion *Diapente*: When therefore the best *proportioned Soul is joyned to the best proportioned body*, it is manifest, that such a man
also

also hath received a most happy lot in the distribution of gifts, For as much as the soul agrees with the body, in the disposition of Naturals, which agreement indeed is most hid, yet after some manner shadowed to us by the wise.

But to hasten to the *Harmony* of the *Soul*, we must inquire into it by those *mediums* by which it passeth to us (*i.e.*) by celestial bodies and *spheres*, knowing therefore what are the powers of the *soul*, to which the *Planets* answer, we shall by those things, which have been spoken of before, the more easily know their agreements amongst themselves; For the *Moon* governs the Powers of Increasing and Decreasing; the phantasie and wits depends on *Mercury*, the Concupiscible virtue on *Venus*, the Vital on the *Sun*; the Irascible on *Mars*; the Natural on *Jupiter*; the Receptive on *Saturn*; but the Will as the *primum mobile*, and the guide of all these powers at pleasure, being joyned with the superiour intellect, is always tending to good; which intellect indeed doth alwayes shew a pathway to the Will, as a Candle to the Eye; but it moves not it self, but is the Mistresse of her own operation, whence it is called Freewill; and although it alwayes tends to good, as an object suteable to it self; yet sometimes being

being blinded with errour, the animal power forcing it, it chooseth evill believing it to be good.

Therefore Will is defined to be a faculty of the intellect and Will, whereby good is chosen by the help of Grace, and Evill not assisting; Grace therefore which Divines call Charity, or infused love, is in the Will, as a first Mover, which being absent, the whole consent fals into dissonancy; Moreover, the *soul* answers to the *Earth* by *sense*, to the *Water* by *Imagination*, to the *Aire* by *Reason*, to the *Heaven* by the *Intellect*, and the soul goes out into a *Harmony* of them according, as these are tempered in a mortall body.

The wise Plato knowing that the Harmonious dispositions of *bodyes* and *souls* are divers, according to the diversity of the complexions of men, did not in vain use musical sounds and singings, as to confirme the Health of the *body*, and restore it being lost. So to bring the minde to wholsome manners, untill they make a man suitable to the *Celestiall Harmony*, and make him wholy Celestiall; moreover there is nothing more *efficatious* to drive away evill spirits then Musicall Harmony (for they being faln from the *Celestiall Harmony*, cannot endure any true consent

sent, as being an Enemy to them, but fly from it: Bodyes being but thick clouds to *Souls*, and there is no more difference betwixt a *soul* and an *Aereal Genius*, then there is betwixt a *Sword in the scabbard and one out of it*: and that a *soul* is but a *Genius* in the *body*, and a *Genius* a *soul* out of the *body*, yet the soul followes the temperature of the body, and is corrupted and rusted in it.

Chap. XIV.

How the soul separates from the body; and is not stopt in the dead corps, as some would have it? how she can get out of the body, that her Union with her Aerial Vehicle *may be very sudden as it were in a moment? how the soul may be loosned and leave the body, and yet returne to it again by ointments: that souls departed communicate dreams. Apparitions of bodies and unbodied Genii, Of Cap.* Lap *&* Dr. Nic Culpeper *appearing after death; How Naturall and Ordinary it is for Genii to appear? Reasons to perswade the unprejudiced that ordinarily those apparitions that bear the shape and person of the deceased, are indeed the souls of them: That the soul is capable of an Aery and Ætherial body,* *dy,* as well as a terrestiall; and also of sense, pain, pleasure; Of the genious power of changing the temper: Of her Aereal Vehicle, and the shape thereof; That the vehicles of Genii have as much of soled corporeal substance in them as the bodies of them: That the naturall abode of souls departed after death is the Aire: How Dæmons and separate Genii hear and see us at a vast distance, and whence it is that though they may so easily hear or see us, we may neither hear nor see them; Of the Touch, Smell, Taste, and Nourishment of Genii; How they are visible one to another: That they converse in a humane shape the better sort of them; the baser in Bestial; of the Igneous splendours of Genii; How they are made; That the external beauty of the Genii is according to the degree of the inward Vertue of their minds? How Ghosts entertaine one another in the other world; of their conferences Philosophicall and politicall; Of their Religious exercises; Of the pastimes and recreations of the better sort; Whence the Aireal Genii have their food; Of the food and feastings of the better sort of Genii.

Concerning the Actuall and Locall Seperation of the *soul* from the Body, it is manifest to be understood of this *Terrestiall Body*, for to be in such a separate State, as to be where Body or Matter is, is to be out

[of

of the world: The whole univerſe being ſo thick ſet with Matter, or body, that there is not to be found the leaſt vacuity therein. The Queſtion therfore is only, whether upon death the ſoul can paſſe from the Corps into ſome other place; *Belen* and *Salmanaz* ſeeme, to arreſt her there by that generall Law of Nature, termed the Law of immortality, whereby every thing is to continue in the ſame Condition it once was in, till ſomething elſe change it; but the application of this Law, is very groſſely unjuſt in this Caſe.

Mr. *Owen* and ſome other of the *Presbyter Prieſts*, wonder how the *Soul* can get out of the *Body*, being impriſoned and lockt up in ſo cloſe a Caſtle. But theſe ſeem to forget both the nature of the ſoul, with the tenuity of her Vehicle, and alſo the Anatomy of the body; for conſidering the Nature of the ſoul her ſelf, and of matter which is a like penetrable every where, the *Genius* can paſs through ſolid *Iron* and *Marble*, as well as through the ſoft *Aire* and *Æther*, ſo that the thickneſſe of the body is no impediment to her; beſides her *Aſtreall Vehicles* is of that tenuity, that it ſelf can as eaſily paſſe the ſmalleſt pores of the body, as the light does Glaſſe, or the lightning the ſcabbard of a ſword *without tearing or scortching of it;* and lastly whether we look upon that principall seat of the plastick power the heart, or that of perception the brain: when a Man dyes, the soul may collect her self, and the small residue of *Spirits* (that may haply serve her in the inchoation of her new *Vehicle*) either in the heart; whence is an easy passage into the Lungs, and so out of the mouth, or else into the head, out of which there are more doores open then I will stand to number. These things are very imaginable, though as invisible as the *Aire*, in whose element they are transacted.

How the soul may live and act separate from the body, may be easily understood out of what has been spoken, but that she does, *de facto,* there are but two wayes to prove it; the one by the testimony of History, the other by Reason; that of History is either of Persons perfectly dead, or of those that have been subject to *Ecstasies,* or rather to that height thereof, which is more properly called ἀφαίρεσία, *when the soul does really leave the body, and yet returne again*; Of this latter sort are the *Rosie Crucians,* who Anoint their heads ἠλεκτρώδῃ φαρμάκω, *with a Gummy Medicine* made of the *Oyle of Ravens, Swallowes, Æther, Gold, Hony, Salt, Mercury,* &c. and this

this would loofen the foul and quit it from the body, and carry it up and down through the world, and fhew it all things, whilft the body, lies *Steaming and sweating, as if it were Purged with fire, &c.*

But the paffing of the foul out of the body in fleepe, or ecftafie, may be fometimes a certaine difeafe, as well as that of the Νυκτοβάται, thofe that walk in their fleep: Now if it fhould happen that fome fuch diftemper fhould arife in the body, as would very much change the vitall cognity thereof for a time; and in this *Paroxcifme* that other difeafe of the *Noctambuli* fhould furprife the party; his *Immagination* driving him to Walk to this or that place, his *Soul* may very eafily be conceived in this loofned condition it lies in, to be able to leave the body, and paffe in the Aire, as other inhabitants of that Element do, and act the part of feparate *Spirits*, and exercife fuch functions of the perceptive faculty, as they do that are quite releafed from terreftriall matter; Only here is the difference, that that Damp in the body that loofned the Union of the foul being fpent, the foul by that *Naturall Magick* I have ufed to difcourfe of in my *New Method of Rofie Crutian Phifick*, will certainly return to the body, and unite with it again as firm as ever, but no men but *Rosie Crucians* can passe out of their bodies, when they please.

The Example of the other sort, *viz* of the appearing of the *Ghosts of Men* after death, are so numerous and frequent in all mens mouths, that it may seem superfluous to particularise in any, This appearing is either by dreams or open visions, in Dreams as that which hapned Ισλία τῆ Βασιλίδι, to *Julia* the Queen; to whom an armed Knight suggested in her sleep, the death of *Appolonius Tyaneus*, and the comming again of her inchanted Servant *Leonides the Second*, her dearly beloved; and it came to passe,

I will adjoyne only three examples or four of Visions, which are ordinarily called apparitions of the Dead, as that of *Nero* (who after the Murdering of his Mother: was haunted with *Demons*, and *Otho* was pulled out of his bed by the *Ghost of Galba*: And a Maid that lived in the house with my Mother, one night was pulled out of her bed by one *John Stringer*, that a little before was killed by one *Richard Evens*, who loved this maid as well as he, and the maid, notwithstanding three doors being lockt fast, had the right side of her haire and headcloaths clean shaved or cut away.

Such instances as these are infinite, I heard
wonderfull

wonderfull delightful Mufick in the Air 100 *miles from any Land,* upon the twelfth of *June,* 1650. Afterwards a gentleman in our Ship being a sleep at noon in the *Cabin,* was called for by a voice from the shore, which hayl'd our ship, few of us took notice of his Name; he was twice called for before any of our men could remember we had any such man aboard; at last he was waked and came upon the deck, and gave a signe that he attended to the Voice; but after giving expresse attention, a clear and distinct voice was heard from the shoare; which was the Desart Island of *Chrisly* in Turkey, uttering these words; *Edward Walford, your Master Nicholas Sheldon is here, when you come into Italy ship speedily home, for your Mistress wishes for you*: At his return he found all this to be truth, for his Master dyed about the houre of that day he heard the Voice.

And my Father *Francis Heydon* with one Mr. *Blackmore* in the year 1644. beheld the hand of *Almighty God, with a sword drawn and shaking it over the West,* it appeared wonderfull glorious with part of the Arm, very fearfull and furious, it was in its motion striking every way all that night, and a few dayes after they heard *Essex* and his Army were routed by the Angel of Almighty God: for so they concluded, Rebellion was punished.

And one Captain *Lap* being merry at our house, told my *Father* and *Mother*, *he would never see them more untill the King came to his throne againe*; *and then he would requite their loves to him, if he lived, and if he dyed, yet he would come and sound a Trumpet unto them*; which in truth he did at a garden doore, and then they remembred his words, and thought he was dead, as suddenly after they heard.

Another Example is of Mr. Doctor *Nich. Culpeper*, whose *Ghost* appeared to his *Widdow*, *Alice Culpeper*, and spake to her, in the *lively Image of his deceased body*, bidding her vindicate him, for he was abused by some *Bookesellers*; He appeared to a fellow in his house, named, *Thomas Harrington*, and gave him a paper, which is now published, wearing the title of Mr. *Culpepers Ghost*, giving seasonable advice to the Lovers of his Writings, and sold by *Peter Cole*, in *Corn-hill*, neer the Royal Exchange, *London*; these Apparitions are really the souls of the Deceased, and no *Devils*, as some fondly conceive, as you may read in the Book.

Now the *Genius* in her *Aerial Vehicle* is capable of sense properly so called, and consequently of pleasure and pain; for there is a necessity

necessity of the resulting of sense from vital union of the *Genius* with any body whatsoever; and we may remember, that the immediate instrument of sense, even in the earthly body, are the spirits; so that there can be no doubt of this Truth. And pleasure and pain being proper modifications of sense, and there being no body but what is passible, it is evident that these *Vehicles of aire* are subject to *pain* as well as *pleasure*, in this Region, where ill things are to be met with as well as good.

And there is as much matter or body in one consistency as another; As for example, There is as much matter in a *Cup of Aire*, as in the same Cup filled with Water, and as much in this Cup of Water, as if it were filled with Lead or Quicksilver, which I take notice of here, that I may free the imagination of men from that ordinary and Idotick misapprehension, which they entertain of Spirits that appear; as if they were as evavid and devoid of substance, as the very shadows of our bodies, cast against a Wall, or our *Images* reflected from a *River* or *Looking-glasse*, and therefore from this Errour, have given them names accordingly, calling the *Ghosts* of men that present themselves to them. Ἐίδωλα & *Umbræ, Images and Shades.* The which, the more visible they are, they think them the more substantial, fancying that the Aire is so condensed, that there is not onely more of it, but also that simple there is more matter or substance, when it appears thus visible, then there was in the same space before: And therefore they must needs conceit that death reduces us to a pittifull thin pittance of being; that our Substance is in a manner lost, and nothing but a tenuous reek remains, no more in proportion to us, then what a sweating Horse leaves behinde him, when he Gallops by in a frosty morning; which certainly must be a very lamentable consideration to such as love this thick and plump body, and are pleased to consider how many pounds they out-weighed their neighbour the last time they were put in the Ballance together.

But if a kinde of dubious transparency will demonstrate the deficiency of corporeal substance, a *Pillar of Chrystal* will have lesse thereof, then one of *Tobacco smoake*; which though it may be so doubtfull and evanid an object to the Eye, if we try it by the hand, it will prove exceeding solid: As also these *Ghosts*, *Genii*, or unbodied Souls, call them which you will, that are said to appear in this manner, have proved to them that

have

have touched them, or have been touched by them. For it is a thing rediculous and unworthy of an *Astronomer*, *Astrologer*, *Geomancer* or *Phylosopher* to judge the measure of corporeal matter, by what it seems to our sight; for so *Ayre* would be nothing at all; or what it is to our handling, or weighing of it; for so indeed a *Cup* of *Quickesilver* would seem to have infinitely more matter in it, then one filled with *Aire* onely, and a vessel of *Water* lefs when it is plunged under the *Water* in the River, then when it is carried in the *Ayre*; but we are to remember, that let matter be of what confistency it will, as thin & pure as the flame of a Candle; there is not lesse of corporeal Substance therein, than there is in the same dimensions of *Silver*, *Lead* or *Gold*.

Seeing its demostrated that Genii have solid bodies, and the place of the *Soul* or *Genius* abode is the *Aire*, and the *Vehicles* of the *Genii* or *Souls* deceased is the *Aire*; nor can the *Souls Vehicle be* incommodated by storms of Winde; and yet *Rain*, *Haile*, *Snow* and *Thunder* will incommodate her lesse: For they passe as they doe through other parts of the Aire which close again imediately, and leave neither wound nor scare behinde them: Wherefore all these Meteors

Master

Mr. *John Gadbury* speaks of, may in their mediocrity be a pleasure to her and refreshment; and in their excesse no long pain, nor in their highest rage any destruction of Life at all: From whence we may safely conclude, that not onely the upper Region, but this lower also, may be inhabited both by the deceased *Souls* of Men and by *Dæmons*. And though we cannot see these *Aerial Spirits*, yet they may not misse of seeing us; and that it may be, from a mighty distance, if they can transform their Vehicle, or the Organ of sight, into some such advantageous Figure, as is wrought in Dioptick Glasses, which power will infinitely exceed the contracting and dilating of the pupill of our Eye; which yet is a weaker and more defectitious attempt towards so high a priviledge as we speak off; which notwithstanding may seem very possible in spirits, the same may be said of their hearing: For the same principle may enable them to shape themselves Organs, for the receiving of sounds, of greater Art and Excellency, than the most accurate acconstick we read of, or can excogitate: Wherefore it is a very childish mistake to think that because we do not every day see the shape, nor hear the discourse of Spirits, that they neither hear
nor

nor see us: For soft bodies are impreſſible by hard ones, but not on the contrary; as melted wax will receive the ſignature of the ſeal, but the ſeal is not at all impreſſed upon by the Wax. And ſo ſolid a body will ſtop the courſe of Aire, but the Aire will not ſtop the courſe of a ſolid body, and every inconſiderable terreſtrial conſiſtency will reflect light, but light ſcarce moves any terreſtrial body out of its place, but is rebounded back by it; that therefore that is moſt tenuious and thin is moſt paſſive; and therefore if it be once the Vehicle of ſenſe, is moſt ſenſible whence it will follow, that the reflection of light from Objects being able to move our Organs that are not ſo fine, they will more neceſſarily move thoſe of the *Genii,* and at a greater diſtance; but their bodies being of *Diaphanous Aire,* it is impoſſible for us to ſee them, unleſſe they will give themſelves the trouble of reducing them to a more terreſtriall Conſiſtency, whereby they may *reflect Light*; nor can we eaſily hear their ordinary ſpeech, partly becauſe a very gentle Motion of the Aire will act upon their Vehicles, and partly becauſe they may haply uſe the finer and purer part of that Element in this Exerciſe, which is not ſo fit to move our ſenſe: and therefore unleſſe they will be heard *da-*

tâ operâ, naturally that impresse of the *Aire* in their usuall discourse can never strike our Organ.

And that we may not seem to say this for nought, that they will have hearing as well as seeing, appears from what I have intimated above, that this faculty is ranged near the *Common Sensorium* in the Vehicle, as well as in that of sight; and therefore the *Vehicle* being all *Aire*, such percussions of it as cause the sence of sound in us, will necessarily do the like in them; but more accurately, haply if they Organize their *Vehicle* for the purpose, which will answer to the arrection of the ears of animalls, for the better taking in the sound.

And they have the sense of touch, else how could they feel resistance, which is necessary in the bearing of one body against another, because they are impenetrable? And to speak freely, my thoughts, it will be a very hard thing to disprove that they have not something analogicall to *Smel* and *Taste*, which are very neare of kin to *Touch* properly so called. For *Fumes* and *Odours* passing so easily through the *Aire*, will very Naturally insinuate into their *Vehicles* also: which fumes, if they be groser and humectant, may raise that Diverfification of touch, which we
Mortals

The Harmony of the World. 189

Mortalls call Tasting: if more subtle and dry, that which we call *Smelling*, which if we should admit, we are within modest bounds, as yet in Comparison of others: as *Cornelius Agrippa*, who affirms down right that the *Arial Genii* are Nourished, and *Cardan* sayes so too, and some of them get into the bodyes of Animalls to batten themselves therein their *blood* and *spirits*, which is also averred by *Zadich*, who tells us that the purer sort of *Genii* are Nourished by drawing in the *Aire*, as our spirits are in the *Nerves* and *Arteries*, & that other *Genii* of a courser kinde, suck in moisture, not with the mouth as we doe, but as a sponge does water: and *Almadir* Writes concerning the *Zabii*, that they eat of the blood of their Sacrifice, because they thought it was the food of the *Dæmons* they worshipped, and that by eating thereof, they were in a better capacity to communicate with them, which things if they could be believed, that would be no such hard probleme concerning the bodies of Spirits and Souls departed.

It is certain that *Genii* and *Ghosts* of *Men*, have the *sence* of *Hearing*, *Seeing* and *Touching* and not improbably of *Smelling* and *Tasting*, which faculties being granted, they need not be much at a losse, how to spend their time,

time, though it were upon externall objects: all the Furniture of Heaven and Earth, being fairly expofed to their view; they fee the fame *Sun* and *Moon* that we do, behold the perfons and converfe of all men; and if no fpeciall Law inhabite them, they paffe from *Town* to *Town*, and from *City* to *City* as *Hyprocrates* alfo intimates.

'Ἥρα ἐκάμενοι πᾶσαν φοιτῶσιν ἐπ' αἶαν.

There is nothing that we enjoy but they may have their fees out of it; *fair fields, large and invious Woods, pleafant Gardens, high* and *healthfull Mountains,* where the pureft gufts of Aire are to be met with, *Chriftall Rivers,* Moffy *Springs, folemnity of Entertainments, Theatrick Pomps* and *Sheaves;* publick and private difcourfes, the *Exercife of Religion,* whether, in *Temples, Families,* or *hidden Cells,* They may be alfo (and haply not uninterreffed) fpectators of the glorious and mifcheivous hazards of *Warr,* whether Sea Fights or Land Fights; befides thofe foft and filent, though fometimes no leffe dangerous, combats in the *Camps* of *Cupid;* and a thoufand more particularities, that it would be too long to reckon up, where they haply are not meer fpectators, but abettors, as *Cardan* Writes: Like *old men* or *Country Parfons* that are paft *Wreftling,* pitching the *Bar;* or *playing at Cudgels*
them-

The Harmony of the World.

themselves, yet will assist and abet the young men of the parish at those Exercises. So the *Souls* of men departed, though they have put off, with the body, the capacity of ordinary functions of humane life; yet they may assist and abet them, as pursuing some designe in them; and that for evill or good, according as they were affected themselves, when they were in the body.

And whatsoever is the custome and desire of the *Genius* in this life, that sticks and adheres to her in that which is to come, and she will be sure, so far as she is capable, either to act it, or to be at least a spectatour and abettour of such kinde of actions; and the better sort of Souls, who having left the body, are *ipso facto* made *Genii* instead of men; that besides the peculiar *hapinesse and blisse* they reap thereby to themselves, they are appointed by God, and have a mission from him, to be Overseer of humane affaires: but that every *Genius* does not perform every Office, but as their natural inclination and customes were in this life, they exercise the like in some manner in the other: And *Tritemius* therefore will have *Æsculapius* to practise Physick, and *Belen* is his Authour (who sayes) *Hercules* is to exercise strength; *Pluto* his *Phylosophy*, *Amphilocus* to Prophecy, *Pytha-*
goras

goras to teach the miſtery of the *Tetractis*, *Æſop* to tell tales, *Caſtor* and *Pollux* to Navigate, *L. Lamius*, *Cœlius*, *Tuberò*, *Confidius*, *Gabrenus*, *Tindorus*, *Palacy*, *Thalia* being dead, were raiſed to life again ; ſo was *Virgil*, *Jaſon*, and a *Spaniſh Earle* ; and theſe *Genii* will aſſiſt mortals to raiſe and revive the dead they ſay.

Thus we read in Hiſtories, many were by *Phyſitians* and *RoſieCrucians* raiſed from death again, as *Juba* and *Xanthus*, *Phyloſtratus*, *Abavis*, *Tillo*, *Tai cum veu huamti*, *Apollonius*, the *Tyanean*, *Zartla* and *Enoch* were by the herb *Dragon-wort*, *Oyle of Gold*, mixt with a medicine made of *Honey* revived : Now *Minos* has Commiſſion in the other world, and is aſſigned to hear Cauſes, and *Achilles* to War.

And there are thirty thouſand immortal *Genii* living on the Earth, which are the keepers of mortal Men, who that they might obſerve Juſtice and mercifull deeds, having cloathed themſelves with Aire, go every where on the Earth : For there is no Prince nor Potentate could be ſafe, nor any Woman continue uncorrupted, no man in this vally of ignorance could come to the end appointed by *God*, if *good ſpirits* did not ſecure us; or if evill ſpirits ſhould be permitted to ſatisfie the wils of men.

The Harmony of the World.

As therefore amongst the *good Genii*, there is a proper Keeper or *King*, deputed to every one, corroborating the spirit of the man to good; so of evill Spirits, there is sent forth an *Enemy*, ruling over the flesh, and desire thereof; and the good spirit fights for us, as a preserverer against the enemy and flesh: Now man betwixt these contenders is the middle, and left in the hand of his own counsel; to whom he will give victory; we cannot therefore accuse *Angels*, if they doe not bring the *Nations* intrusted to them to *Episcopal Government*, and the knowledge of the *true God, to true piety*, and suffer them to fall into *Errours* and *Anabaptisme*, *perverse worship* and *Presbytery*; but it is to be imputed to themselves, who have of their own accord declined from the right path, adhearing to the spirits of Errour, giving victory to the *Devill*: For it is in the hand of Man to adhear to whom he please, and overcome whom he will; by whom, if once the Enemy, the *Devill* be overcome, he is made his servant; and being overcome, cannot fight any more with another, as a Wasp that hath lost his sting.

And these spirits appear variously clad; some like *beautifull Virgins*, others like *valiant Warriours*, with their *Helmets*, and *plumes of Feathers*;

Feathers; as *Achilles* did to *Appolonius*; and *Eugenius Theodidactus*, speaking of *Genii* or Separate soules, make them all to appear in humane shape, as you may read in these verses; where he and his fellows are going to converse with them, and thus he sayes they carryed him.

To Babylon *my swift course I apply,*
Where once arriv'd, I chance to cast my eye
On a Caldean *grave, but in his Art*
Miraculous, compleat in every part; (long
His haire mixt white, his beard both full and
Of venerable aspect, (*for i'le not wrong,*
His presence) *and to tell you true his Name*
Mythrobarzanes: *Unto him I came,*
Humbly entreating, but with much ado,
My earnest suit he would give ear unto;
Though I then promised him sufficient hire
To path the way, I did so much desire;
At length he yeilds, *then instantly new coyns me,*
And for full five and twenty days enjoyns me
Just as the Moon (*as near as I can guesse*)
Begins to Bath her self in Euphrates,
To wash with her, each morning early then,
He to a place conducts me, where and when
I must expose me to the Suns uprise;
When mumbling to himself in a strange guise,

A

The Harmony of the World. 195

A tedious deal of Stuff (but bad or good
I knew not, for no part I understood)
As foolish Cryers I have known, so he
Speak at high speed, his Volu'ble tongue was free
Without deliberate period, not a word
Certain, or least distinction did afford:
It seems he invok'd some dead Ghost to the place
That charm being done, he strook thrice on the
So brought me back again without more let(grasse;
Turning his eye upon no man he met.
Our food was onely Mast dropt from the Oke,
We had to drink when thirst did us provoke,
Milk, Wine with Honey mixt (a liquor good
With Water new drawn from Choaspes flood,
Saving the grasse, we had no other Bed.
Our bottles and our scrips thus furnished,
And we so victualled, in the dead of Night
To Tygris flood he guided me forth right,
There I was washt again and dryde) a Brand
He kindled then, such as I understand
They use in purging Sacrifice; then takes
Up a Sea Onion, and of that he makes
(With like ingredients) a most strang confection
Mutt'ring again, for more safe protection
His former, antic verse, inchanting round
The circled place in wch we then were bound,
And next he compast me with many a charm,
Least I from fearfull Sp[ec]tors should take harm:

O 2   Then

Then brought me back, having made preparation
In the Nights last part, for our Navigation;
An Exercised robe (such as the Medes
Are us'd to weare) he then puts on, and leads
Me to his Wardrobe, and there furnisht me
With this disguised habite that you see,
Namely a Lyons skin, a club and lyre,
Charging me, that if any should desire
To know my Name, I and by no means should say,
I was Eugenius, and my self betray:
But either the faire-spoken man Ulysses,
Cromwell, or the great club-man Hercules.
Mythro. Resolve me yet more plainly friend where
This forraign habit with thy change of name came
Eu. Ile make't perspicuous, Thus much he intended
If I like those who living had descended
Before our times, my self could truly shape;
I might perhaps th' inquisitive eyes Escape
Of Eacus, and so have free admission
In a known habit, without prohibition.

The day appear'd, the lake we having entred
And through a glomy vault our selves adventred
For he had all things ready there, the Barge,
The Sacrifice, the mixt Wine, and the charge
Of each concealed mystery that needed;
All these being safely stow'd, we next proceeded
To place our selves, both full of tears and sad;
Yet through the flood we gentle passage had,

And

The Harmony of the World.

And in short space to a thick Wood we came,
Much like a wildernesse, and in the same
A lake, in which deep Euphrates is hid,
That likewise past as our occasions bid,
We anchor'd in a Region, where we view'd
Nothing but Trees, darknefs and solitude.
Where landing (for my guide conducted still)
We dig a pit first, then fat Sheep we kill, place:
And with their luke-warm blood besprinkle the
Now the Chaldean after some smal space,
Kindles again his brand, whispers no more,
But with a clamorous voice aloud 'gan rore,
And invocates those Dæmons, such as we
Call Pænæ, Erinnes, Tochot & Mild mægeles;
Who in the Night hath power next Proserpine;
And with their dreadfull names doth interline
Words, many-syllabl'd, of obscure sense,
Barb'rous, absurd, deriv'd I know not whence;
These spoke confusedly, Crannies appear'd,
Through which the hidious yelling throats were heard
Of Cerberus, ev'n Orcus seem'd to shake
And frighted Pluto, in his Throne to quake:
Straight many places to be gaz'd upon
Lay ope to us, as Perephlegeton,
With many spacious Regions. Sinking next,
Stern Rhadamant, with terrour almost dead
Now from his Kennel, where the Dog lay spread,
Cerberus rous'd himself and barkt; when I
This Harp into mine hand took instantly,

Q 3   And

And with my voice and strings such measure kept,
The cur was charm'd, therewith sunk down & slept:
When to the Lake for waftage we were come,
No passage we could get for want of room,
The Barge had her full frieght of wretched souls,
In which was nothing heard save shrieks & houls;
For all these Passengers had woulded been,
Some in the breast, some in the thigh and skin;
And in some one or other member; all
These in a late fought battle seem'd to fall.
But Excellent Ess-x when he saw me clad
In these rich Lyons spoiles, a great care had
To have me plac'd unto mine own desire;
Then wafted me without demanding hire,
Mistaking me for Cromwell. And when
We toucht the shore, he was so kinde agen,
As point us out the way. Black darknesse now
Involv'd us round, neither discern'd I how
To place one foot; but catch hold of my guide,
And follow'd as he lead, us fast beside
(Through which we past) a spacious medow was
More full of daffodilies than of grasse:
Here many thousand bodies of men dead
With humming noise were circumfus'd and spread,
Still following us; On still we forward trudge,
Untill we came where Minos sate as Judge
In a sublime tribunal; on one hand
The pains and furies, and the tortures stand,

With

The Harmony of the World.

With the evill Genii : *On the oppofite fide
Were many pris'ners brought, in order ty'de
With a long Cord; and thefe were faid to be*
Accus'd for killing of the King, by crueltie.
And Bauds, Baliffs, Cutthroats, Lyllians *& fuch
As in their life time had offended much;
And of thefe a huge rable. Now a part
from thefe appear'd, with fad and heavy heart,*
Rich men and Ufurers, migre lookt & pale,
Swoln-bellyed, gouty-legg'd, *each one his gaile
About him had, being faftned to a Beame,
Barr'd and furcharged with the weight extream
Of two main pondrous talents of old* Iron :
Now whileft thefe pris'ners Minos *Seat inviron
We ftanding by,* &c.

Thus have I fhewed that *Genii* converfe in humane fhape, yet they are fometimes vifible to us, under fome *Animal fhape,* which queftionleffe is much more difficult to them then that other vifibility is : But this is alfo poffible, though more unufuall by farr, as being more unnaturall. For it is poffible by Art to *compreffe Aire* fo, as to reduce it to *vifible oparity,* and has been done by fome of my *Pupiles;* the Aire getting this oparity by fqueezing the *Globuli* cut of it: which though the feparate *Souls* and *Spirits* may do by that dereƈive faculty, yet furely it would be very painfull. For the firft Element lying
bare,

bare, if the *Aire* be not drawn exceeding close, it will cause an ungratefull heat: and if it be, as unnaturall a cold: and so small a moment wil make the firstElement too much or too little, that it may haply be very hard at least for these inferiour spirits, to keep stedily in a due mean. And therefore, when they appeare, it is not unlikely but that they soak their *Vehicles* in the vaporous glutinous moisture the *Rosie Crucians* speak off, that they may become visible to us at a more easy rate, and alwayes the better sort appeare in humane shape.

As it is likely also that those Θιοπτίαι or αὐγαὶ πυρώδεις, those *Igneous splendours Artesius* make mention of (as the end and scope of these *wicked wretches*; he describes) often used were coloured according to the more or lesser ferulency of the *Vehicle* of the *Dæmon* that did appeare in this manner, *viz.* in no personall shape, but by exhibiting a light to the eyes of his abominable spectators and adorers, which, I suppose he stirred up within the Limits of his own *Vehicle*; the power of his will and Immagination, commanding the grosser particle of the *Aire* and *terrestriall* vapours; together with the *Globuli*, to give back every way, from one point to a certain compasse, not great, and therefore the more
easy

easy to be done. Whence the *first Element* lies bare in some considerable measure, whose activity cannot but lick into it some particles of the *Vehicle* that borders next thereto, and thereby exhibit, not a pure *Starr-light* (which would be, if the first element thus made naked or uncloathed, and in the midst of pure *Aire*, were it self unmixt with other matter) but the ferulency of those parts that it abrades and converts into fewel, and the foulnesse of the *Ambient Vehicle* through which it shines, makes it look *red and fiery* like the *Horizontall Sun*, seen through a *thick throng of vapors*, which *Fiery Splendour* may either onely slide down amongst them, and so passe by with the motion of the *Dæmons Vehicle*, which *Cardan* seems also to aime at; or else it may make some stay and discourse with them it approches, according as I have heard; some Narrations out of *Jamblious*; the reason of which lucid appearances being so intelligible out of *Phioates the Indian Prince* and the *Rosie Crucian Philosophy*; we need not conceipt that they are nothing but the prestigious delusions of Fancy and no reall object, as the Learned Mr. *John Gadbury* and Mr. *John Booker* would have them; it being no more uncompetible to *Dæmon* to raise such a light in
his

his *Vehicle*, and a purer then I have described, then to a wicked man to light a Candle at a tinder box.

For though there be neither lust, nor difference of sex amongst these *Genii* (whence the kindest commotion of minde will never be any thing else, but an exercise of intellectuall love, whose object is vertue and beauty;) yet it is not improbable, but that there are some generall strictures of discrimination of this beauty into *Masculine* and *Feminine*: partly, because the temper of their *Vehicles* may encline to this kinde of pulchritude rather then that; and partly because severall of these *aeriall spirits* have sustained the difference of *sex* in this life; some of them here having been *Males*, others *Females*: and therefore their History being to be continued from their departure hence, they ought to retaine some Character; especially so generall a one, of what they were here; And it is very harsh to conceit, that *Frost* will meet Mr. *Lilly*'s Wife in the other world, in any other forme then that of a Woman: Although not with so much pleasure there as here; Whence a necessity of some slighter distinction of habits, and manner of wearing their haire will follow, which dresse, as that of the Masculine Mode, is easily fitted to them

them by the power of their will and immagination.

Now the immediate instrument of the *soul* in this life is the *spirits*, which are very congenerous to the body of *Angels*, and that all our passions and conceptions are either suggested from them, or imprest upon them; he cannot much doubt, but that all his faculties of *Reason*, *Imagination* and *Affection*, for the generall, will be in him in the other state, as they were here in this, namely that he will be capable of *Love*, of *Joy*, of *Grief*, of *Anger*; that he will be able to imagine, discourse, to remember, and the rest of such opperations as were not proper to the fabrick of this earthly body, which is the officine of death and generation.

And the Animall life is as essentiall to the Soul as Union with a body, which she is never free from; it will follow, that there be some fitting gratifications of it in the other World. And none greater can be immagined then sociablenefs and personall complacency, not only in the rationall discourses, which is so agreeable to the *Philosophical Ingeny*, but innocent pastimes, in which the *Musicall* and *Amorous propension* may be also recreated. For these three dispositions are the flower of all the rest, as *Swarez* has somewhere

where noted: and his reception into the other world is set out by *Sabrinus*.

Μεθ' ὁμηγύρειν ἔρχεαι ἤδη
Δαιμονίω ἐξουσίοισιν ἀναπνεύσαν αὔταις.
Ἔνθ' ἔνι μὲν φιλότης, ἔνι δ' ἵμερος ἀβρὸς ἰδέσθαι
Εὐφροσύνης πλείων καθαρῆς πληρόμερος αἰέν
Ἀμβροσίων ὀχετῶν θεόθεν· ὅθεν ὅπιν ἐρώτων
Πείσματα κ̀ γλυκερὴ πνοιὴ νήνεμος αἰθήρ.

Id Est.

Now the blest meeting you arrive unto
Of th' airy Genii, where soft winds do blow,
Where friendship, love, and gentile sweet desire,
Fill their thrice welcome guests, with joys entire;
Ever supply'd from that immortall spring ; (bring
Whose streams pure Nectar from great Jove do
Whence kinde converse and amorous Eloquence,
Warms their chast minds into the highest sense
Of Heavenly Love, whose mystries they declare
'Midst the fresh breathings of the peacefull Aire.

Now this *Blisse* the fancy consults with, the first exemplar of beauty, intellectuall love and vertue, and the body is wholy obedient to the immagination of the minde, and will to every *Punctilio* yield to the impresses of that inward patterne; nothing there can be found amiss, every touch and
stroake

stroake of motion and beauty being conveyed from so Judicious a power, through so delicate and depurate a *Medium*. Wherefore they cannot but *enravish* one anothers *Souls*, while they are *mutual spectators* of the perfect pulchritude of anothers persons, and *comely carriage*, of their gracefull *Dancing*, their melodious *Singing* and *playing*, with *accents so sweet and soft*, as if we should imagine the *Aire* here of it self to *compose lessons*, and send forth *Musicall sounds* without the helpe of any *terrestriall instrument*. These and such like passetime as these, are part of the happinesse of the best sort of the *Aireall Genii*.

The food of the bad Genii is *vaporous Aire*, formally made up into dishes by the power of immagination upon their own *Vehicles*, first dabled in some humidities, that are the fittest for their designe, which they change into the forme of viands, and then withdraw when they have given them such a *figure, colour* and *consistency*, with some small touch of such a *Sapour* or *Tincture*.

But these superiour Dæmons, which inhabit that part of the *Aire*, that no storm nor tempest can reach, need be put to no such shifts, though they may be able in them as the other :. For in the tranquility of those upper Regions, that *promus Condus* of the U_
niverse

niverſe, *the ſpirit of nature* may ſilently ſend forth whole *Gardens* and *Orchards* of moſt *delectable fruits* and *flowers* of *Aquilibrious pondoroſity* to the parts of the *Aire* they grow in, to whoſe *ſhape* and *colours* the tranſparency of theſe plants may add a particular luſtre, as we ſee it is in precious Stones. The very ſoile is tranſparent, in which you may trace the very roots of the Trees of this ſuperiour *Paradice* with your Eyes, and not offend them; ſee this Opake Earth through it: Nay the *Sapheric Earth*, bounding your ſight with ſuch a white ſplendour, as is diſcovered in the *Full Moon*, with that difference of brightneſſe, that will ariſe from the diſtinction of *Land* and *Water*; and if you will recreate your palates, may taſte of ſuch fruits, as whoſe natural juice will vie with their nobleſt *extractions* and *Quinteſſences*. For ſuch certainly will you there finde; *the blood of the Grape*, the Rubie coloured *Cherries*, and *Nectarineſſe*; and if for the compleating of the pleaſantneſſe of theſe habitations, that they may look leſſe like *ſilent* and dead *ſolitude*, you meet with *Birds* and *Beaſts* of curious ſhapes and *colours*, the *ſingle accents of whoſe voyces are very gratefull to the eare*, and the varying of their Notes perfect *the Muſical Harmony, &c.*

Chap.

Chap. XV.

That there is a Political Order and Laws amongst the Aiery Dæmons; *That this* Chain of Government reaches down from the highest Ætherial powers, through the Aerial to the very Inhabitants of the Earth ; *the peculiar feature and individual Character of the Aerial Vehicle* ; *The retainment of the same name* : *How to finde the Names of Genii* : *A Table* : *What kinde of punishments the Aerial Officers inflict upon their Malefactours ? What mischeif men may create to themselves in the other World by their zealous mistakes in this, the unspeakable torments of Conscience, worse than death, and not to be avoided by dying* : *Of the spirit of Nature, what it is ? That the sympathy betwixt* the Earthy *and* Astral body *argue its existence*; *The roundnesse of the Sun and Stars prove it* : *An absolute demonstration of the existence of the Spirit of Nature , its grand Office of transmitting souls into rightly prepared matter* : *Of the seldome appearing of Spirits* ; *Of the tragical pompe and dreadfull preludes of Death, with some corroborative considerations against such sad spectacles* : *What may befall the Genius, and the hazards she runs after this life* ;

life; whereby she may again become obnoxious to death: That the Æthereral Vehicle instates the Genius *in the everlasting* blisse and happinesse, *&c.*

I Shall next speak to you of the *Policy* of the *Aiery Genii*, concerning which ; that in general there is such a thing among them, I have proved *in my Idea of the Law*, *the second Book*, to be the most assuredly true in it self, and of the most use to us to be perswaded of; to know their particular Orders and Customes is a more needlesse curiosity : But that they doe lie under the restraint of *Government*, is not onely the opinion of the *Pythagorians* (who hath even to the nicity of Grammatical criticisme, assigned distinct names to the Law, that belongs to these three distinct ranks of beings, ἄνθρωποι, δαίμονες & Θεοὶ, calling the law that belongs to the first Νόμ⊕, the second Δίκη, and the third Θέμις, but it is also the easie and obvious suggestion of ordinary Reason, that it must needs be so, and especially amongst the *Aerial Genii* in these lower Regions, they being a mixt rabble of good and bad, wise and foolish, in such a sense we may say, the inhabitants of the earth are so; and therefore they must naturally fall under a *Government*, and submit

The Harmony of the World.

mit to *Law*, as well and for the same Reasons as men do. For otherwise they cannot tollerably subsist, nor enjoy what rights may some way or other appertain to them, for the *souls* of *Men* deceased and the *Dæmons*, being endued with corporeall sense, and therefore capable of pleasure and paine, and consequently, of both injury and punishment, it is manifest, that having the use of reason, they cannot faile to mould themselves into some *politicall* forme or other, and so to be divided into Nations and Provinces, and have their *Kings, Princes, Dukes, Earles, Lords; Knights, Esquires,* and *Officers* of *State, Judges, Serjeants, Counsellors, Recorders, Secundaryes, Phillizers, Prothronitores, Barresters Clerks, Atturneys, Solicitors, Justices* of *Peace, Constables, Head Borrowes* and all others, to the very lowest and most abhorred *Executioners of Justice Bayliffs, &c.*

Which invisible *Government* is not Circumcised within the compasse of the *Aiery Regions*, but takes hold also of the Inhabitants of the Earth, *as the Government of men* does on severall sorts of Beasts, and the *Etherial* powers also have a right & exercise of Rule over the *Aiereall*; whence nothing can be committed in the world against the more indispensible *Laws* thereof, but a most severe and

P   inevitabel

inevitable punishment will follow: every Nation, City, Family and Person, being in some manner the *Peculium*, and therefore in the tutellage, of some invisible power or other, as I have afore spoken of:

It is not impertinent to my purpose, to take notice also, that the naturall and usuall figure of the Souls, *Aerial Vehicle* bears a Harmonious resemblance with the feature of the party in this life; it being most obvious for the plastick part (at the command of the will, to put forth into personall shape) to fall as near to that in this life, as the new State will permit, with which act the spirit of nature haply does concurr, as in the Figuration of the *Fœtus*: but with such limits as become the *Aerial Congruity of life*, which I said before; as also how the proper *Idea* or *Figure* of every *Soul* (though it may defect somthing by the power of the parts, Imagination in the act of conception, or Gestation yet may return more neare to its peculiar semblance afterwards, and so be an unconcealable note of indivisibility.

In the Flesh there is three thousand *Angels* that keep and preserve mortall men (as I said in the last Chapter) their names you shall finde by this Table following entring with some sacred, Divine or *Angelicall* name,

in

in the collumn of letters defcending: by taking thofe letters which you fhall finde in the common Angels under the *Stars* and *Signes:* which being reduced into order, you will finde the name and nature of your *good Angell*; by the example of my Nativity, I fhall name fome for example-fake, viz. *Malhircel, Monadel, Chavakiah, Lehahiah, Jehujah, Vafariah, Lerabel, Omael, Reijel,) Seebiah, Jerathel, Haajah, Nithbaiah, Hahuiah,* Melahel, *Jejajel, Nelchael, Pahaliah, Leuviah, Vehuiah, Jeliel, Sirael, Elenuah, Mahafiah, Lelahel, Achacah, Cahethel, Haziel, Aladiah, Lauiah, Habajah, Mebahel, Haziel, Hakimiah, Caliel, Aniel, Rehael, Sealiah, Ariel, Afaliah, Imamiah, Nanael, Nithael, Mebahiah, Poiel, Nemamiah, Hararel, Nizrael, Umabel, Jahhel, Anavel, Mehekieh, Damabiah, Eivel, Meniel, Habuiah, Jibamiah, Mumiah, Hajajel,* &c. And there be three thoufand *Dæmons,* in the worft fenfe that feek whom they may devoure, its neceffary, now for your better underftanding hefe things; that you read my *Temple of Wifdome* being a book of *Geomancy, Aftrology* nd *Telefmes.*

For you muft know that every man hath a three fold *good Dæmon,* the firft is *holy,* the other is of the *Nativity,* and the other is of the *rofeffion* the holy *Dæmon,* is affigned to the ationall *Soul* by the *Idea.*

Darkness	☽ ♋	☿ Ⅱ ♍	♀ ♉ ♎	☉ ♌	♂ ♈ ♏	♃ ♐ ♓	♄ ♑ ♒	
z ת א	ו	ו	ה	ד	ג	ב	א	a
x ש φ	נ	ס	ל	כ	י	ט	ח	b
v ר υ	ש	ר	ק	צ	פ	ע	ס	c
t ק τ	ו	ה	ד	ג	ב	א	ת	d
s צ σ	מ	ל	כ	י	ט	ח	ז	e
r פ ρ	ר	ק	צ	פ	ע	ס	נ	f
q ע π	ה	ד	ג	ב	א	ת	ש	g
p ס ο	ל	כ	י	ח	ז	ו	h
o נ ξ	ק	צ	פ	ע	ס	נ	מ	i
n מ ν	ד	ג	ב	א	ת	ש	ר	k
m ל μ	כ	י	ט	ח	ז	ו	ה	l
l כ λ	צ	פ	ע	ס	נ	מ	ל	m
k י κ	ג	ב	א	ת	ש	ר	ק	n
i ט ι	י	ט	ח	ז	ו	ה	ד	o
h ח θ	פ	ע	ס	נ	מ	ל	כ	p
g ז η	ב	א	ת	ש	ר	ק	צ	q
f ו ζ	ט	ח	ז	ו	ה	ד	ג	r
e ה ε	ע	ס	נ	מ	ל	כ	י	s
d ד δ	א	ת	ש	ר	ק	צ	פ	t
c ג γ	ח	ז	ו	ה	ד	ג	ב	v
b ב β	ס	נ	מ	ל	כ	י	ט	x
a א α	ת	ש	ר	ק	צ	פ	ע	z
Hatred	♄ ♒	♃ ♐ ♓	♂ ♈ ♏	☉ ♌	♀ ♉ ♎	☿ Ⅱ ♍	☽ ♋	

of God, through the *Starrs* and *Planets*, and this doth direct the life of the soul, and doth alwayes put good thoughts into the minde, being alwayes active to illuminate us, and if you would know his *Name*, you must enter *the line of Light*: For by this *Spirit* you may avoid the Malignity of a fate, and the *Genius* of the *Nativity*, doth descend from the *disposition of the Anima of the world*, & from the *Circuit* of the *Starrs*, which were powerful in his *Nativity*, and when the soule comes down from Almighty *God*, into the body, it doth out of the Quire of *Angels*, naturally choose a preserver to it self, & not onely choose this guide to it self, but hath that willing to defend it. This being the Executor and Keeper of the life, doth help it to the body, and takes care of it, being communicated to the body, and helps a man to that very Office, to which the Cœlestials have deputed him being born of men *Genii*.

For when you have found the names as Authors, Teach and Write, you will easily finde the Angels that Governs that name; For *Jupiter* and the *Sun* signifies *John*; *Mercury* and *Mars*, *Matthew*; the *Sun* *Stephen*; if the *Sun* be principal significator, *James*; if *Letitia*, *Abraham*; if the *Moon* and *Mercury*, *Simon*, if *Tristitia*, *Benjamin*; if *Jupiter* and *Sol*, *Clement*;

Clement, Rubacus, Cornelius; if Mercury, Charls' Albus, Daniel; Mercury and Saturn, Edmund, Fortuna Minor, Escanius; if Aries, Edward; Saturn and Venus, William; Mars and Sol, Robert Taurus, Joseph, Mars and Sol, Peter; Caput Draconis, Giles; Gemini, Philip; Fortuna Major, Francis; Mars, Anthony; Cauda Draconis, Henry; Sol and Mercury, Benjamin; Cancer, Gideon, Puella, Jacob; Jupiter and Saturn, Thomas; Leo, Paul, Puer, Kenelme; Sol, Roger; Virgo, George, acquisitio, Michael; Libra, Leonard; Saturn and Sol, Gregory, Amissio, Nicholas; Scorpio, Oliver; Sol and Saturn, Andrew via Petalinus; Sagitarius, Quintilliam; Moon and Sun, Hercules, Carcer, Ralph; Capriconus, Sampson; Moon and Saturn, Nicholas, Populus, Tristram; Aquarius, Eustace; Jupiter and Sun, Richard; Pisces, Jonathan; Conjunctio, Bernard: Note also, among the Planets, Signes and Figures of Geomancy, that any name may be found out besides those which we have written, according the Planets, Signes and Figures you finde upon the Angles; And Lætitia may signifie Adam, as if the corners of the Figure consent, and so of the rest, as you may see by the Numbers of Figures and signes in my *Temple of Wisdome*.

The Harmony of the World.

♂	✱	□	△	♄
o	t	v	a	i
a	e	i	o	v

To underſtand this, you muſt according to the experienced Rules of Authors, ſee your ſignificator or ſignificators of the party enquired of; whether he be Angular or no, and whether he be in Aſpect with any Planet or Figure; and as of the one, ſo muſt underſtand both; and if there be no Aſpect, then conſider whoſe Dignities he is in; As for example, Let us admit *Sol* Lord of the ſeventh, and ſignificator of Theft, or what you enquire after, and he in the Dignities or Aſpect of *Saturn*, I ſhould then ſay the parties name is *Andrew*.

Now you know how to finde the name of all things, any party by *Geomancy* and *Aſtrology*, if you would next know the name of his *Genius* you muſt they ſay, as is proved by experience, know the *Genius* of the Planet or Star, which is Lord or Lady of Birth, or chief in the Figure of Geomancy, or hath moſt dignities or from that into whoſe houſe the *moon* was to enter, after that which at the birth of the man it doth retain: ſome finde it from the Sun and Moon, some from the Angles; some fortifie the Eleventh house with a good Planet Figure, and get a Genius, which therefore they call a good Demon; but an evill Genius from the Sixth.

Now you must note every signe in 30. degrees, and what Letter you finde upon the first Degree of *Aries*, fals upon the second degree of *Taurus*; and if the Letters be not compleat, you must add some name of Divine Omnipotency, as *Os, El. Jod, On Jah*, &c. but the name *Ell*, because it imports power and virtue; is therefore added not onely to good but bad spirits; for neither can evill spirits either subsist, or do any thing without the virtue of *El God*; and you must observe the Harmony of the Signes, Planets, Stars and Figures of Geomancy.

♈

1	2	3	4	5	6	7
A	B	C	D	E	F	G
8	9	10	11	12	13	14
H	I	K	L	M	N	O
15	16	17	18	19	20	
P	Q	R	S	T	V	
21	22	23	24	25	26	26
W	X	Y	Z	El	Ris	Os
28	29	30				
Jah	On	Jod				

Now *B.* is attributed to the first degree of *Taurus*, *C.* to the first of *Gemini*, *D.* to the first of *Cancer*, and *E.* to the first of *Leo*, &c.

And if you enter *the left-hand* it is for evil, you will finde the name of that *lying spirit*, the tempter or enfnarer of you; but you have liberty to yeeld to whom you pleafe, &c. but to come to the *foule* in the *Aireal Region*, where I left her; we will there give her the fame name which the deceafed had here, unleffe there be fome fpecial reafon to change it; fo that their perfons will be as punctually diftinguifht, and cirucmfcribed as any of ours in this life: All which things, as they are moft probable in themfelves, that they will thus naturally fall out; fo they are very convenient for adminiftration of *Juftice*, and *keeping of order in the other State*: and thus we finde her name.

In the Table, before you are taught how to calculate the names of *Genii*, good and bad under the prefidency of the Seven *Planets*; and thefe cœleftial *Angels are fervants of the ftars*; as the ftars are guided by their Angels, and as man is guided by his fpirit; now thofe of the lower order may be procured and conveyed to us, and all thofe on the right hand are good and entring, and of the

Element

Element of *Fire* and *Aire*: And if you enter the Table on the left side, those are evill and going out, and of the Element of the *Water* and *Earth*; yet if you finde by your Figures of *Geomancy* and *Astrology* the nature of your *Genius* to be Watery or Earthly by the signes of the Angles and Aspects, on the right hand it is good; And if on your left you enter, and finde a Figure of the *Fire* or *Aire*, it is evill, because you enter on the left hand: And as there is a *Harmony* of the *Heavens*, so there is a harmony of the *Elements* in their mixions as Earth becomming dirty, being dissolved becomes water, and the same being made thick and hard, become Earth again; but being inaporated through heat, passeth into Aire, and that being kindled, passeth into Fire; and this being extinguished, returns back again into Aire, but being cooled again after its burning, becomes earth, or stone, or sulphur; and this is manifested by Lightning: Now the Earth never changes, but relents and is mixed with other Elements, which do dissolve it, but it returns back into it self again; but their qualities are these, Fire is hot and dry, Earth dry and cold, Water cold and moist, the Aire moist and hot; Earth and Water are heavy, Fire & Aire are Light, which make

The Harmony of the World.

make this Active, and yet Paſſive; and again, there are three other qualities aſſigned to every one of them, *viz*. to the Fire, Brightneſſe, thinnes and Motion, but to the Earth, Darkneſs, Thickneſſe & Quietneſſe; now the other Elements borrow their qualities from theſe; ſo that the Aire receives two qualities of the Fire, thinneſſe, motion, and one of the Earth, *viz*. Darkneſſe; The Water receives in like manner, two qualities of the Earth, darkneſs and thickneſſe, and on the Fire, *viz*. motion; but Fire is twice more thin than Aire, thrice more movable, and fouretimes more bright.

And the Aire is twice more bright, thrice more thin, and four times more movable then Water; wherefore Water is twice more bright then Earth, thrice more thin, and four times more moveable: As the Fire is to the Aire, ſo Aire to the Water, and Water to the Earth; and again, as the Earth is to the Water, ſo the Water to the Aire, and the Aire to the Fire: Now by this Table following, and Sixteen Figure, viz. *Aquiſitio, Albus, Populus, via, Conjunctio, Carcer, Fortuna major, Puella, Puer, Fortuna minor, Amiſſio, Lætitia, Rubeus, Triſtitia, Caput Draconis, Cauda Draconis*, of the Earth or Geomancy, they foreknow future things by the motions of the Earth; by noiſe ſwelling

swellings, tremblings, chops, pits, exhalations and other impressions of points, which have a certain power in the fall of them; as the *Idea's* and Spirits guide them to this or that: Now you must know that the *Earth* and *Water* live, as well as *Fire* and *Aire*; for of themselves they generate, vivifie, nourish and increase innumerable Trees, Plants and living Creatures; as most manifestly appeares in things that breed of their own accord, and in those which have no corporeal seed; and these are generated by the soul of the Earth, or Water, and these soules have reason, is apparent; for whereas the universall works of the aforesaid soules doe with a perpetual order conspire amongst themselves, it is necessary that they be governed not by chance but by reason; by which reason they doe direct, and bring all their operations to a certainty: For it is necessary that the Earth should have the Reason of terrene things, and Watery of Watery things, &c. by which reason, each in their time, place and order, are generated, but being hurt, are repaired, and the perfection of a body is its soul; And it is said, a man staying long under Water, was taken up dead, but by letting him blood he revived again We read of *Virgil* a *Spanish* Earle, *Aniela*, *Gabienus*, *Tubero*, and a certain
Babylonian

Babylonian that were dead, whom they say, beyond all expectation, the *Physitians* with *Draggon wort* restored to life; others say they were restored by *Honey in a Medicine*: Now there are signes given, whereby it may be known who are alive, although they seem to be dead, green and stink; and indeed will dye unlesse there be means used to recover them; And this is the manner we understand *Rosie Crucians raise the dead*: Now they raise *Birds, Dogs, Horses, Flowers* otherwise, by burning their bodies to Ashes, and then restore them to life. And again, you must understand, as every Region in the Cœlestials hath a certain *star* and *cælestial image*, which hath influence upon it before others: so also in supercœlestials doth it obtain a certain intelligence set over it, and guarding it with infinite other ministring Spirits of its order, which are all called *Sons of the God of Hosts*.

But evill Spirits doe wander up and down in this inferiour world, enraged against all, whom they therefore call *Devils*; of whom St. *Austine* in his first Book of the Incarnation of the word to *Januarius* saith: Concerning the Devil and his Angels, contrary to vertues the Ecclesiastical preaching hath taught; that there are such things: but what they are and how they are, he hath not clear enough expound-pounded? Yet there is this opinion amongst most, that this *Devill* was an Angel, and being made an Apostate, perswaded very many of the Angels to decline with himself, who even unto this day are called his Angels. The *Church* notwithstanding thinketh not that all these are damned, nor that they are all purposely evill, but that from the Creation of the world, the *Dispensation* of things is ordained by this means, that the tormenting of sinfull soules is made over to them; The *Cardinals of Rome* say, that not any Devil was created evill, but that they were driven and cast forth of *Heaven*, from the orders of good Angels, for their Pride, whose fall not onely our *Bishops, Divines, and Hebrew Theologions*, but also the *Assyrians, Arabians, Ægyptians* and *Greeks* doe confirm by their Tenents.

Every man hath a good and a bad spirit attends him, and a threefold good *Genius*, as a proper keeper or preserver, the one whereof is holy, another of the nativity, and the other of profession, the *Holy Genius* is one according to the Doctrine of the *Rosie Crucians* assigned to the rationall soul, not from the Starrs or Planets, but from a supernaturall cause, *from God himself the president of Genii*, being universall above nature: This doth direct the life of the soul, and doth alwayes
put

put good thoughts into the minde, being alwayes active in illuminating us, although we do not take notice of it; but when we are purified, and live peaceably, then it is perceived by us, then it doth speak with us, and communicate its voice to us being before silent, and studying dayly to bring us to a Sacred perfection, also by the aid of this Genius we may avoid the malignity of a fate; now the Genius of the Nativity, doth here descend from the disposition of the world, and from the circuits of the Stars and Planets, which were powerfully dignified in the Nativity; & there be some say when the soul is comming down into the body, it doth out of the quire of the Angels naturally chose a preserver to it self, nor only choose this guide to it self, but hath that willing to defend it, this being the exemptor, & keeper of the life doth help it to the body, and helps a man to that very office, to which the celestials have deputed him being borne; the Genius of profession is given by the Stars, to which such a profession, or sect, which any man hath professed, is subjected, which the soul when it began to make choice

The Harmony of the World.

The Harmony of the World.

In this body, and to take upon it self, difpofitions, doth fecretly defire; when therefore a profeffion agrees with our Nature, there is prefent with us a Genius of our profeffion like unto us, and futable to our Genius; As having my felf *by the profeffion of the Law* a Genius, which makes my life more peaceable, happy and profperous; but when we undertake an unlike or contrary to our Genius, our life is made laborious and troubled with difagreeing Patrons.

In the firft place, know your good Genius and your Nature, and what good the celeftial and terreftrial difpofitions promife thee, and God the diftributer of all thefe, who diftributes to each as he pleafeth, and follow the beginnings of thefe profeffe thefe, be converfant in that virtue to which the moft high diftributor doth elevate, and lead thee, who made *Abraham* excell in juftice and clemency, *Ifaac* with fear, *Jacob* with ftrength, *Mofes* with meekneffe and miracles, *Joſhua* in war, *David* in Religion and Victory, *Solomon* in knowledge, *Julius Cæfar* in fame, *Plato* in divine learning, *Peter* in Faith, and *John* in Charity: Therefore in what virtue you think you can moft eafily be a proficient in, ufe diligence to attain to the height thereof; that you may excell in one, when in many you cannot, but in the rest, endeavour to be as great a proficient as you can; these Genii being found, they will sometimes speak with an audable voice, as they that cryed at the Ascention of *Christ*, *Ye men of* Galile, *why stand ye hear gazing into the Heavens*: The names of some of these are of great virtue against diseases, some cure all, and some obtain efficacy and virtue to draw any spiritual substance from above or beneath, for to make any desired effect   I have seen a name written upon Virgin Parchment at a certain time, and afterward given to be devoured by a Water-Frog, being let go into the water, rains & showers presently followed. And they finde in the table of the twelve Militant signes and sixteen Figures of the Earth, the name of a Genius, & seal it with his seal, which I saw inscribed at a certain houre, & given to a Crow, who being let go presently, there followed from that corner of the Heaven, whether he flew, lightnings, shakings and horrible thunders, with thick clouds: It is not lawfull for me to write what secret I know, least it should happen that the sacred name should be abused by prophane men to base things: but if they desire the knowledge of them, let them so often turn the Letters, and examine them

untill

untill the voice of God is manifest: Let us go unto another principle.

If any be so curious as to demand, what kinde of punishment this people of the *Aire* inflict upon their Malefactours, I had rather refer them to *Psellus Plotinus*, *The Auditor of Anebo* and *Cornelius Agrippa*, then descend to such particularities, They say, the *Caverns of the earth* are made use of for Dungeons for the wicked *Dæmons*, to be punished in; as if the several *Volcano's*, such as *Ætna*, *Strumbulo*, *Hecla*, *Mongebel*, *Vesuvius*, the *Gulph of Persia*, where they say *Judas* hail's all ships that saile upon those Seas, and tels them, there he is punished for betraying his *Lord and master Jesus Christ, the Son of God, &c.*

That there is a tedious restraint upon them, for villanies committed, and that intollerable, is without all question; they being endued with *corporeal sense*, and that more quick and passive than ours; and therefore more subject to the highest degrees of torment: So that not onely by incarcerating them, and keeping them in by a *Watch*, in the *Caverns of burning mountains*, where the heat of those Infernal *Chambers*, and the steam of Brimstone cannot but excruciate them exceedingly, but also by commanding them into sundry other hollows of the ground, noisome by several Fumes and Vapours, they may torture them in several fashions and degrees, fully proportionable to the greatest crime that is in their power to commit, and far above what the cruelty of that worst of *Tyrants*, *Oliver Cromwell* has inflicted here, either upon the guilty or innocent. But how these confinements & torments are inflicted on them, and by what degrees and relaxations, is a thing neither either to determine, nor needfull to understand: Wherefore we will surcease from pursuing any further, so unprofitable a subject, and come to the third general head, we mentioned, as being most *Harmonical* to our discourse, which is, what the *morral condition* of the soul is, when she has left this body.

These things therefore premised, it will not be hard to conceive, how the condition of the *Soul* after this life, depends on her moral deportment here; for *memory ceasing not, Conscience may very likely awaken* more furiously then ever, the mind becoming a more clear *Judge* of evill actions past, then she could be in the *Flesh*, being now stript of all those circumstances of things that kept her off from the opportunity of calling her self to account, or of perceiving the uglinesse of her own wayes.

Besides

Besides, there being that communication and *Harmony* betwixt the *Earth* and the *Aire*, that at least the fame of things will *arive* to their cognifcance that have left this life; the after ill fuccesse of their wicked enterprifes, and unreasonable tranfactions may arm their tormenting Confcience, with new Whips and stings, when they fhall either hear or fee with their Eyes, what they have unjuftly built up, to run with fhame to ruine; and behold all their defignes comes to nought, and their fame blafted upon Earth.

This is the ftate of fuch foules as are capable of a fenfe of diflike of their paft actions. And a man would think they need no other punifhment then this, if he confidered the mighty power of the Minde over her own *Vehicle*, and how vulnerable it is from its felf. Thefe Paffions therefore of the *Genius* that follow an ill Confcience, muft needs bring her *Aiery body* into intollerable diftempers, worfe than *Death* it felf.

Nor yet can fhe dye, if fhe would, neither by *Fire* nor *Sword*, nor any means imaginable; no not if fhe fhould fling her felf into the flames of *fmoaking Ætna*; for fuppofe fhe could keep her felf fo long there, as to endure that hideous pain of deftroying the vitall Congruity of her *Vehicle* by that Sulphurus fire: She would no sooner be released, but she would catch life again in the *Aire*, and all the former troubles and vexations would return; besides the overplus of these pangs of Death. For *Memory would return, and an ill Conscience would return, and all those busie Furies*; those disordered passions which follow it. And thus it would be, though the *Genius* should kill her self, ten thousand times she could but pain and punish her self, not destroy her self.

I had now finished this Chapter, did I not think it convenient to speak of the spirit of Nature, which is a substance incorporeal, but without sense and animadversion, pervading the whole matter of the Universe, and exercising a plastical power therein, according to the sundry predispositions and occasions in the parts it works, upon raising such *Phanomena* in the world, by directing the parts of the Matter and their Motion, as cannot be resolved into meere mechanical powers: And I prove there is such a spirit by the sympathy betwixt *Astral* and *Earthly bodies*; for the *Genii* of men leaving their bodies, and appearing in shapes, *suppose of Cats, Pigeons, Conies, Stars, flames of Fire*, sometimes of *Men*, and that whatsoever hurt befals them

them in thefe *Aftral bodies*, the fame is inflicted upon their terreftrial; lying in the mean
time in their *Beds* or on the ground.

As if their *Aftral bodies* be fcalded, woun-
ded have the back broke, the fame certainly
happens to their *earthly bodies*; And thus the
fpirit of *Nature* is fnatcht into confent with
the *imagination of the Genii in thefe Aftral bodies*
or *Aeiry Vehicles*, which act of imagination
muft needs be ftrong in them; it being fo fet
on, and affifted by a quick and fharp pain,
and fright in thefe fcaldings, woundings and
ftroaks on the back; fome fuch thing hap-
pening here, as in women with childe,
whofe fancy made keen by a fudden feare,
have deprived their children of their Arms,
yea and of their heads too.

And this fpirit of *Nature* directs the motions of the *Ætherial Particles* to act upon thefe
groffer bodies, to drive them towards the
Earth: for that furplufage of agitation of
the *Globular particles* of the *Æther*, above what
they fpend in turning the *Earth* about, in
Harmony to the *heavens* is carried every way
indifferently, according to his own conceffi-
on; by which motion the drops of liquors
are formed into round Figures; from whence
it is apparent, that a *Bullet of Iron, Silver, or*
Gold

232 *The Harmony of the World.*

Gold, placed in the Aire, is equally affalted on all fides by the occurfion of thefe *ætherial particles,* and therefore will be moved no more downwards then upwards; but hang in *æquilibrio,* as a peice of Cork refts on the water, where there is neither winde nor ftream, but is equally played againft by the Particles of water on all fides.

I fhall demonftrate what I have faid, that heavy bodies in the very clime where we live, will not defcend perpendicularly to the Earth, and this will be evident to the Eye

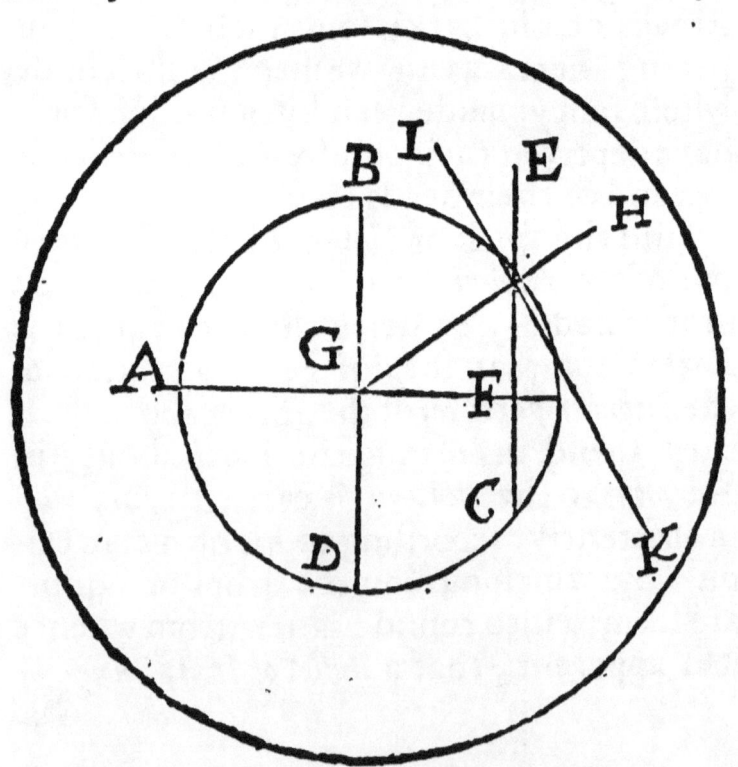

and to Reason, that the proportion of their declination from a perpendicular in any Elevation of the Pole : In the Circle there *A. B. D.* let the Æquator be *S.D.* and from the point *C.* draw a line to *E* parallel to *B. D.* which line *C E.* will cut the Circle in *F* sixty degrees, suppose from *B* let a heavy body be now at *E.* according to Mr. *Streets* Hypothesis, it must fall towards the Earth in a line parallel to the Æquator, *viz* in the line *E F.* And thus he disputed with me some years since, to prove the Earths Mobility: but his Solution of the Problem is very dry. The Earth moves, I do not deny ; but I wish he could argue or Reason it better, for say I, *E. F.* declines from the line *H.F* drawn perpendicular to the Horizon *L. K.* two third parts of a right angle, (*i e.*) 60. degrees For the *E. F. H.* is equall to *C F.K.* which again is equall to the alternate angle *B.G.F* which is two third parts of a right angle *ex thesi*, whence it is plain that *E. F.* declines from a perpendicular no lesse than 60. degrees. By the same reason, if we had drawn the scheam for the Elevation of 50. which is more souther then our Clime, I might demonstrate that the descent of heavy bodies, declines from a perpendicular to the *Horizon* 50. degrees, or five ninthes of a right angle, &c.

From

From whence it will follow, that men cannot walk upright, but declining, in the elevation suppose of 60. degrees as neer to the ground as *E.F.* is to *F L.* and much neerer in the more remote parts of the North; and there is proportionably the same reason in other Climes, if we draw a Scheam for the parallel, under which we live, suppose about 52. degrees of Elevation we might represent truly to the Eye, in what posture men would walk upon the *Royal Exchange, London, Oxford,*

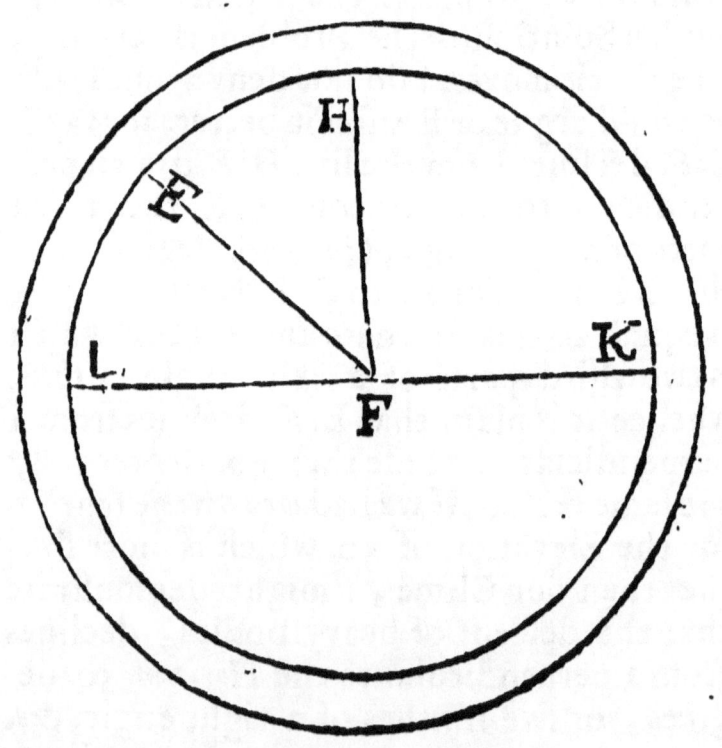

Warwick-Castle, Alsester, Colton Parke, Tardebick Church, Worcester, Bristol, St. *Peters* Churchyard in *Exeter*, in *Sydmouth*, in *Salisbury* Cathedral, or in *Westminster*-Hall, &c. For it is plain from what hath been above demonstrated, that the natural posture of their bodies upon the *Horizon L. K.* it would be in the line *E. F.* out of which, if they did force themselves in the line *H. F.* without being born head-long to the ground, and laid flat upon the Horizon, *F K.* the force of the Aire or whatsoever more subtle Elements therein pressing in lines parallel to *E. F.* and therefore necessary bearing down whatsoever is placed loose in the line *H. F.* as is plain to any at first sight.

Add unto all this, that if the motion of grosse bodies were according to meer Mechanical laws; a Bullet, suppose, of Lead or Gold, cast up into the Aire, would never descend again, but would persist in a rectiliner motion, for it being far more solid than so much *Aire* and *Æther* put together, as would fill its place, and being moved with no lesse swiftnesse then that wherewith the *Earth* is carryed about in twenty four houres, it must needs break out in a streight line through the thin *Aire*, and never return again to the *Earth*; but get away as a Commet does out

of a

of a *Vortex*. And that *defacto*, Col. *John Knotsford* at a Garrisons of the Kings, shot a Canon bullet so high, that it never fel back again upon the ground; now the spirit of Nature at a certain distance leaves the motion of matter to the pure laws of Mechanicks, but with in other bounds checks it; whence it is that the water does not swill out of the *Moon*.

Now the most notable of those Offices that can be assigned to the *Spirit of Nature*, and that sutable to his name, is the translocation of the souls of Beasts into such Matter as is most fitting for them, he being the common *Proxinet* or *Contractor* of all natural Matches and Marriages, betwixt Forms and Matter; For *Materia appetit formum ut fœmina virum*, this spirit therefore may have not onely the power of directing the Motion of Matter at hand, but also of transporting of particular Souls & Spirits in their silence, and in activity to such matter as they are in, a fitnesse to catch life in again: which transportation or transmission may be very well at immense distances, the effect of this sympathy, and coactivity being so great in the working of the *Wines* in *England*, when the *Vines* are in the Flower at the *Canaries*, *Tenneriff*, *Medera*'s or any place in *Spain*, &c.

When

Whence to conclude, we may look upon this *spirit of Nature*, as the great *Quarter-master* general of *Divine Providence*, but able alone, without any under Officers to lodge every *soul*, according to her rank and merit, when ever she leaves the body: And would prove a very serviceable Hypothesis for those that fancy the pre-existence of humane soules, to declare how they may be conveyed into bodies here, be they at what distance they will before; and how matter haply may be so fitted, that the best of them may be fetcht from the purest *Ætherial Regions* into an humane *Body*, without serving any long *Apprentiship in the intermediate Aire*: As also how the souls of *Brutes*, though the Earth were made perfectly inept for the life of any animal, need not lie for ever uselesse in the Universe.

Now I say the *Genii* of *Men*, being in the same condition that other *spirits are*, appear sometimes though but seldome: The cause in both being, partly the difficulty of bringing their *Vehicles* to an unnatural consistency, and partly their having no occasion to doe; and lastly, it being not permitted to them to doe as they please, or to be where they have a minde to be.

Methinks this *Tragick pompe* and *Harmony* looks mournfully, preparing to die, laying
waste

waste all the operations of the Mind, putting her into fits of dotage and fury, making the very Visage look ghastly and distracted, and at the best sadly pale and consumed; as if life and soule were even quite extinct, cannot but imprint strange impressions even upon the stoutest minde, and raise suspitions that all is lost in so great a change But the knowing and benigne spirit, though he may flow in tears at so dismall a spectacle, yet it does not at all suppresse his hope and confidence of the *Genius*'s safe passage into the other world, and is no otherwise moved then the more passionate spectators of some cunningly *contrived Tragedy*; where persons whose either *virtue or misfortunes*, or both, (*for they seldome part*) have woen that affection of the beholders, are at last seen wallowing in their blood, and after some horrid groans, and gasps, lye stretcht starke dead upon the stage

But being once drawn off, find themselves well and alive, and are ready to taste a cup of Wine in the Attyring room with their friends; to solace themselves really, after their Fictious *pangs* of *Death*, and leave the easie multitude to indulge to their soft passions, for an evill that never befell them.

The

The fear and abhorrency therefore we have of *Death*, and the sorrow that accompanies it, is no argument, but that we may live after it, and are by due affections for those that are to be Spectators of the great *Tragick Comedy of the World*; the whole plot whereof being *an Harmony of the Spheres, Planets* and *Influenciary beams*, being contrived by *Infinite Wisdome and Goodnesse*, we cannot but surmise that the most sad representations are but a shew, but the delight real to such as are not *wicked and impious*; and that what the ignorant call evill in this Universe, is but as the shadowy stroks in a faire Picture; or the mournfull notes in Musick, by which the beauty of the one is more lively and expresse, and the melody of the other more pleasing and melting.

I have now conducted the soul into the other state, and installed her into the same condition with the *Aerial Genii*, but seeing that those that take any pleasure at all in thinking of these things, can seldone command the ranging of their thoughts, within what compasse they please, and that it is obvious for them to doubt whether the *Genius* can be secure of her permanency in life in the other world, (it implying no contradiction, that her vital congruity, appropriate to

this

this or that Element, may either of it self expire, or that she may by some carelesse debilitate one congruity, and awaken another in some measure; so make her self obnoxious to fate) we cannot but think it in a manner necessary to extricate such difficulties as these, that we may not seem in this aftergame to loose all we woon in the former.

The *Genius* after the death of the body runs through three hazards, one respects an intrinsecal *principle*, the *periodical* terms of her vital congruity, or else the Levity and miscarriage of her own will, which obnoxiousnes of hers is still more fully argued from what is affirmed of the *Aerial Genii* (whose companion and fellow Citizen she is)whom sundry Phylosophers assert to be Mortal; and that she is revolved hither thrice, and no more; because this number seems sufficiently to suffice, for the purgation of sins, as you may read in my *Rosi Crucian infallable Axomata lib.2. chap. 4.* at large; the other two hazards she runs, are from without, *to the Conflagration of the world*, and the *Extinction of the Sun*.

Now whether the *souls of men* be *virtuous or vitious*, they *must* dye to *their Aerial Vehicles*, which seems a sad story at first sight, as if Righteousnefs could not deliver from death; but if it be more carefully perused, the terrour

rour will be found onely to concern the wicked. For the profoundest pitch of death is the defcent into this terreftrial body, in which, befides that, we neceffarily forget whatever is paft, we do for the prefent lead ἀλαμπῆ ᾗ ἀμυδρὴν ζωὴν, a dark and obfcure life, dragging this weight of Earth along with us, as *Traitors* and *Malefactors* doe their heavy Fetters in their feclufe confinements.

But in our return back from this ftate, life is naturally more large to them that are prepared to make good ufe of that advantage they have of their *Aiery Vehicle*: But if they be not Mafters of themfelves in that ftate, they wil be fatally remanded back to their former prifon in proceffe of time, which is the moft groffe death imaginable. But for the good and *virtuous fouls*, that after many ages change their *Aerial Vehicle* for an *Ætherial one*, that is no death to them, but an higher afcent into life. And a man may afwell fay of an Infant that has left the dark womb of his Mother, that this change of his is Death, as that a *Genius* dyes by leaving the *groffe Aire*, and emerging into that *Vehicle of Light*, which they ordinarily call *Ætherial*.

There may be a dangerous relapfe out of the *Aerial Vehicle into the Terreftrial*, which is properly the death of the *Soul* that is thus

R retrograde;

retrograde. But for those that ever reach the *Ætherial State*, the periods of life there are infinite; and though they may have their *Periges* as well as *Apoge's*, yet these circuits being of so vast a Compass, and their *Perige's* so rare and short, and their return as certain to their former *Apsis*, as that of the *Cœlestial bodies*, and their *Ætherial* sense never leaving them in their lowest touches towards the *Earth*; it is manifest that they have arrived to the life that is justly *called Eternal*. Thus the body returns to the earth from which it was taken, the Spirit returns to the *heavens* from whence it descended, and the Soul or Genius returns to *God* that gave it.

CHAP.

CHAP. XVI.

How the Earth *is consumed, and the bodies of the dead, and what becomes of the dust of those that are resolved into their first Principle; that the conflagration of the earth will prove fatal to the souls of the wicked men and* Dæmons; *what the cursed spirits and souls will suffer, and what be their thoughts that do groan in* Sheol, *when* Minos *judges them:* Eugenius Theodidactus *testimony of the Ayreal state, and five several Opinions more concerning their state after the conflagration, that the Sun being turned into darkness, and the Moon into blood, is no panick fear, but may be rationally suspected from the Records of History, and grounds of Natural Phylosophy, the said influence of this extinction upon man and beast, and all the* Aireal Genii *imprisoned within their several Armospheres in our Vortex, that it will do little or no dammage to the Æthereal Inhabitants, in reference to heat or warmth, nor will they find much want of his light, how they may pass out of one Vortex into another, by the priviledge of their Ætherial Vehicles, without labour or toil, and be safe: that wicked souls and Dæmons will revive again, and that the earth and ayr will be inhabited by them.*

I Have thus inthroned my Genius in her Æthereal Vehicle, where she is a very magnificent thing, full thing, *full of Divine Love, Majesty, and Tranquility*; and shall next consider the condition of the souls of *men* and *Dæmons*, after the *earth* is consumed, for naturally the earth perisheth, by *water*, or by *fire*; and this happeneth every seven thousand *years*, and to the Heavens every 36000 years, as *Winter* and *Summer* do in our ordinary year: *In undatio non secus quam Hyems, quam Æstas lege* Mundi *venit*: But for this ἐκπύδατωσις, it not being so famous, nor so frequently spoken of, nor so destructive, nor so likely to end the world as the other way, nor belonging so properly to my purpose, I shall let it pass: The general *Prognostick* is concerning fire now, not only of the *Stoicks*, as *Zeno*, *Cleanthes, Chrysippus, Seneca*, but of several also of different Sects, as *Heraclitus, Epicurus, Cicero, Pliny, Aristocles, Numennius*, &c.

Seneca sayes the stars will run and dash one against another, and so set all on fire, and consume the earth, and all bodies upon it, or in it, both living and dead: The destroying the *Æthereal* Region, is as foolish a fancy, *as the sentencing of the Eele to be drown'd*, because the matter of the *Æther* is too fine and subtil for fire to rage in, it being indeed nothing but a pure light or fire it self; and yet this *Æthereal matter* is infinitely the greatest portion of the world. Where-

Wherefore the world cannot be said properly to be lyable to the destruction of fire, from any natural causes, as *Lactantius*, *Ireneus*, and the *Stoicks* would have it; for fire is nothing but the motion of certain little Particles of matter, and there is no more motion at one time in the world, then at another, because one part of the matter cannot impress any agitation upon another, but it must loose so much it self: This hideous noyse therefore of the conflagration of the world must be restrained to the firing of the earth only, so far as it concerns us, for there is nothing else combustible in the Universe but the Earth, and other Planets, and what vapours and exhalations arise from them.

And the most certain and most destructive execution this fire will do, must be upon the *unrecovered souls* of *wicked men and Dæmons*: Those that are so deeply sunk and drown'd ως γηινσιν, that the very consistency of their Vehicles does imprison them within the confines of this thick caliginous ayr; these souls or spirits therefore that have so inextricably intangled themselves in the fate of this lower world, giving up all their senses to the momentary pleasures of the moyst luxurious Principle, which is the very seat of death: These in the mystical *Phylosophy* of the *Rosie Crucians*, are the *Nymphs*, to whom though they allot a long *Series* of years, yet they do not exempt them from *Death* and *Fate*; and *Eugenius Theodidactus* pronounces, that their life will be terminated with the conflagration of the world, for thus he intimates, Καὶ ὁ λόγ‿ ὅλ‿ ἠνίχθαι δοκεῖ τῷ Ἡσιόδῳ πρὸς τ̄ ὑκπύρωσιν, ὁπλωίκα συνεκλείπειν τοῖς ὑγροῖς εἰκὶ ὅτι τὰς Νύμφας.

—————— Αἵ τ' ἄλσεα καλὰ νέμονται
Καὶ πηγὰς ποταμῶν ἠ πείσεα ποιήεντα.

And indeed this young *Phylosopher* has pretty fancies, let us hear him in his Mother Tongue, for thus he brings in *Minos* judging the dead: A little after his former verses in the fourteenth Chapter.

Now *Minos* after strict examination,
And justly informed by their accusation,
Contrudes them all unto the sad society,
Of such as are condemn'd for their impiety:
With them incessant torments do endure
A just infliction for their deeds impure:
But against such, he is incensed most,
Who whilst they liv'd did of their riches
 boast:

Whom

Whom dignity and ſtile ſwell'd with oſtent,
Who in their proud hearts, could have been content
To have had adoration; he hates pride,
And doth ſuch haughty inſolence deride,
As ſhort and momentary, becauſe they knowing
Themſelves unto their Marbles hourly growing,
As being mortals; yet in their great glory,
Think not their wealth & riches tranſitory;
But all theſe ſplendours they have now laid by,
Wealth, Gentry, Office, Place, and Dignity,
Naked, ſad-lookt, perplext with grief extream,
Thinking what paſt in life-time a meer dream;
To behold which, I took exceeding pleaſure,
And was indeed delighted above meaſure.
If any of them by chance I knew,
As private as I could, I neer him drew,
Demanded what before was his condition,
And whether, as the reſt, ſwell'd with ambition:
About the door there was a throng of ſuch,
By *Pluto's Miniſters* offended much;
Beaten and thruſt together all about,
Who, as it ſeems, would gladly have got out;

To these he scarcely moving in a *Gown*,
Which from his shoulders to his heels flow'd down,
Of *Scarlet*, *Gold*, and divers colours mixt;
Casting his head that way, on some he fixt
An austere eye; such counting it a *bliss*,
To whom he but vouchsaft a hand to *kiss*;
At which the others murmur'd, *Minos* then
Setling himself upon his Throne agen,
Some things most justly sentenc'd, there appear'd
The Tyrant *Cromwell* evilly chear'd,
Not knowing what excuses for to bring,
Being accus'd *for killing of the King*:
Hewet & *Slingsby* testates to that Conviction,
And he now ready to be doom'd to infliction
With other Traytors, who without repentance,
Have had their Judgement read, and past Sentence.

From the *Tribunal*, we our course extend,
Unto the place of *torments*, where (O friend)
Infinite miseries at once appear,
All which we freely might both see & hear;
Together with the sound of *stripes* & *blows*,
Loud *ejaculations*, *shrieks*, *tears*, *passionate woes*,
Eccho'd from these wrapt in invisible flames,
Wheels, *Racks*, *Forks*, *Gibbets*, to tell all their names,
Not possible. Here *Cerberus* besmears

His

His triple chaps in blood, ravens and tears.
The wretched fouls; the fell *Chimæra* takes
Others in her sharp claws, and 'mongst them makes
A fearful massacre, limb from limb dividing.
Not far from thence in a dark place abiding
Were Captives, *Tyrants*, and Bayliffs, of these store,
And with them mingled both the rich and poor:
These all together and alike tormented,
Who now too late have of their sins repented;
And others of them, whom we beheld and knew,
Who dy'd not long since, such themselves withdrew;
And as asham'd to be in torments seen,
In dark and obscure nooks their shadowes skreen;
Or if they doubtfully cast back their eyes,
Blushes are seen from their pale cheeks to rise,
And only such themselves in darkness shroud,
Who were in life most insolent and proud.
These objects having past, at length we come
Unto the field call'd *Acherusium*.

No sooner there, but streight we hapt a-
  mong
The *Demi-gods*, the *Heroes*, and a throng
Of several *Troops*. ———

But let us take a more serious and distinct view of the condition of the *Genius*, after the conflagration of the earth; and here I meet with five several sorts of Opinions concerning it: *The first hold, that this unmerciful heat and fire will at last destroy and consume the soul as well as the body*: But this seems to me impossible, that any created Substance should utterly destroy another Substance, so as to reduce it to nothing: For no part of matter, acting the most furiously upon another part thereof, does effect that; it can only attenuate, dissipate, and disperse the parts, and make them invisible; but the substance of the *Soul* is indissipable and indiscerpible, and therefore remains entire, whatever becomes of the body or Vehicle. Thus *Virgil*.

Yet the *Bodies* when they die,
Are not cleer'd from all their misery;
They having not repented of their crimes,
Must now be punish'd for their misspent
  times.

The

The second opinion is, *That after long and tedious tortures in these flames, the Soul by a special act of Omnipotency is annihilated*: But methinks, this is to put Providence too much to her shifts, as if God were so brought to a plunge in his creating a creature of it self immortal, that he must be fain to uncreate it again (*i.e.*) annihilate it: Besides, that that *Divine Nemesis* that lyes within the compass of *Phylosophy*, never supposes any such forcible eruption of the Diety into extraordinary effects, but that all things are brought about by a wise and infallible, or inevitable train of secondary causes, whether Natural, or free Agents. And saith the Poet;

Four things of Man there are, *Spirit, Soul,*
   Ghost, Flesh,
These four, four places keep, and do possess
The *Earth* covers *Flesh*, the *Ghost* hovers o're
   the *Grave,*
Orcus hath the *Soul, Stars* do the *Spirit* crave.

The third therefore, to avoid these absurdities, denies both absumption by fire and annihilation; but conceives, that tediousness and extremity of *pain* makes the *Soul* at last, of her self, shrink from all Commerce with Matter, the immediate principle of Union,

nion, which we call *vital congruity*, consisting of a certain modification of the body, or *Vehicle*, as well as of the *Soul*, which being spoiled and lost, and the Soul thereby quite loosened from all sympathy with body or matter, she becomes perfectly dead, and senseless to all things, and as they say, will so remain for ever. But this seems not so rational; for as *Plato* somewhere hath Ἕκαστον, οὗ ἐστιν ἐνέργεια, ἐστιν ἕνεκα τοῦ ἔργυ: Wherefore so many entire immaterial substances would be continued in being to all Eternity, to no end nor purpose, notwithstanding they may be made use of, and Actuate matter again as well as ever. And in another place he hath it:

―――― But for their crimes
They must be punish'd, & for misspent times
Must tortures feel; some in the *winds* are
   hung,
Others to cleanse their *spotted sins*, are *flung*
Into vast *Gulphs*, or *purg'd by fire*.

A fourth sort therefore of speculations there is, who conceive, that after this solution of the *Souls* or *Spirits* of wicked men, and from their *Vehicles*, that their *pain* is continued to them even in that separate state,
                                        they

they falling into an unquiet sleep, full of furious tormenting dreams, that act as fiercely upon their *spirits*, as the external fire did upon their bodies. But others except against this Opinion as uncertain, *viz.* that the Soul can act when it has lost all vital union with the matter, which seems repugnant with that so Intimate and Essential aptitude it has to be united therewith; and the dreams of the Soul in the body, are not transacted without the help of the *Animal Spirits in the Brain*, they usually symbolizing with their temper: Whence they conclude, that there is no certain ground to establish this Opinion upon.

The Souls of the *wicked* will be tortured (saith the fifth) in the other state, with most cruel hatred of imaginary evil, and false suspicions, and most horrible phantasmes that then fall, and there are represented to them most sad things, sometimes of the Heavens falling upon their heads, sometimes of being consumed with violent flames, sometimes of being drowned in a Gulf, sometimes of being swallowed up into the Earth, sometimes of being changed into divers kinds of beasts, sometimes of being torn and devoured by ugly Monsters, sometimes of being carried abroad through Woods,
Seas,

Seas, Fire, Ayr, and through fearful places, wandring sometimes *like Souldiers upon the Sea*, and sometimes like strange *birds*, sometimes like *Maremen* and *Maremaids*, and upon the shore in divers shapes of *men*, *beasts*, and these we call *Satyres, Fauni, Silvani, Nereides Naiades Orcades, Dryades*, and *Dii tutulares* of *Cities* and *Countryes*; and those that love the warmth of Families, and homely converse with men, *Lares Familiares*.

And these things happen to them after death, no otherwise then in this life; to those who are taken with a *phrenſie*, and some other *melancholly* distemper, or to those who are affrighted with horrible things, seeing dreams, and are thereby tormented, as if these things did really happen to them, which truly are not real, but only species of them apprehended in imagination, even so do horrible representations of sins terrifie those souls after death, as if they were in a dream, and the guilt of wickedness drives them headlong through divers places, &c.

Now when the *Sun is turned into darkneſs, and the Moon into blood*, it will be very hideous, and intolerable to all the Inhabitants of the Planets in our *Vortex*, and poor mortals will be wearied with heavy languishments, both for want of the comfort of the

usual

usual warmth of the *Sun*, whereby the bodies of men are recreated, and also by reason of his inability to ripen *the fruits of the foyle*; whence necessarily must follow, *Famine, Plagues, Sicknesses,* and at length an utter *devastation and destruction of both men and beasts*; nor can these *Genii* scape free, but that the vital tye to their Vehicles, necessarily confining them to their several *Atmospheres*, they will be inevitably imprisoned in more then Cimmerian darkness; as the Poet saith.

Here people are that be *Cimmerian* nam'd,
Drown'd in perpetual darkness, it is fam'd,
Whom rising nor the setting Sun doth see,
But with perpetual night oppressed be.

For the darkness of the *Sun* will turn the *Moon into blood*, and put out all the light of the *Stars* and *Earths*, and nothing but *Ice* and *Frosts*, and *flakes of Snow*, and thick mists, as palpable as that of *Egypt*, will possess the Regions of their habitation: But the *Genii* that have arrived to their *Æthereal Vehicle*, can turn themselves into a pure *actual light* when they please, their Region being a soft *milde light*, and but a change of pleasure, as it is to see *the Moon shine fair into a room* after

the

the putting out of the Candle; and these *Æthereal Genii* being now safe, let us look down a little, for all the world is now in a flame; and when the fire has done due execution upon that unfortunate crew, and tedious and direful torture has wearied their afflicted *Ghosts* into an utter recess from all Matter, and thereby into a profound sleep or death, that though those *twinkling eyes of Heaven*, the *Stars*, might be compassionate Spectators, yet they cannot send out one ray of light to succour or visit the earth, their tender and remote beams not being able to pierce, much less to dissipate the clammy and stiff consistency of that long and *Fatal Night*.

Wherefore calling our mind off from so dismal a sight, let us place it upon a more hopeful object, and see what follows this Fate, after a long series of years, when not only the fury of the *fire* is utterly slaked, but that vast *Atmosphere* of smoak and vapours, which was sent up during the time of the *Earths Conflagration*, has returned back in copious showers of *Rain*, which will again make *Seas and Rivers*, will bind and consolidate the ground, and falling exceeding plentifully all over, make the soil pleasant and fruitful, and the *Ayr* cool and wholesome,

some, refreshed again with a *new Heaven, a new Sun, Moon and Stars*; and nature recovering thus to her advantage, and becoming *youthful again*, and full of *Genital salt and moysture*, the *souls* of all living creatures belonging to these lower Regions of the *Earth* and *Ayr*, will awaken orderly in their proper places, the *Seas* and *Rivers* will be again replenisht with *Fish*, the *Earth* will send forth all manner of *Fowls*, *four-footed beasts*, and creeping things; and *the souls of men* also shall then *catch life from the more pure and Balsanick parts of the Earth*, and be cloathed again in *terrestrial bodies*. And lastly, the *Aerial Genii*, that Element becoming again wholesome and vital, shall in due order and time, awaken and revive in the cool rorid ayr, which expergefaction into life, is accompanied with propensions answerable to those resolutions they made with themselves in those *fiery torments*, and with which they fell into their long sleep.

And thus have I demonstrated the *Harmony of the World, mans body*, and the *souls of both*, *from the Creation to the Conflagration*: There are also other *mysteries*, but we shall abundantly discourse of all these in the *following Books*; wherefore we now put an end to the first Book.

S   THE

The Postscript.

THus have I Reader demonstrated the Harmony of the Heavens, and how the Spirits ascend and descend from Earth to Heaven, and from Heaven to Earth: The harmony of beams, and how Spirits and Souls slide down into the bodies; of the harmony of mans body; of the harmony of his Soul, with medicines fitted for the benefit of both: I have conducted the Soul into the place from whence it was conveyed and præ-existed, and now perhaps you do begin to bless your self: For is it possible (say you) that any bodily substance should inclose such mysteries as these? In this, my friend, you have your liberty, I value no mans censure, and therefore trouble not your self about it, for your Faith will add nothing to it, and your Incredulity cannot take any thing from it: This only you shall do, be pleased to give way to my sauciness; for I must tell you, I do not know that which I may call impossible: I am sure there are in Nature powers of all sorts, and answerable to all desires, and even those very powers are subject to us; and I have discoursed of them by way of objection, and answered my own Positions, for the better satisfaction of my Readers: I have discovered my self in arguing known truths,

reserving

The Postscript.

reserving the rest to my self, and those that shall deserve them, being freely willing to do good to my enemies, if I have any, and to the envious, following the example of Christ, the King, and the Bishops; for my soul fears God, honours the King, and loves the Bishops, and their forms of Government, hoping this little Book will be to them as I am, free from discord : But some not content, (because they never heard of what I have written) think this but my fancy and invention, and no practical truth; take notice of these Authors, Gentlemen, and they will testifie for me, viz. God, and these his created servants, Moses, Zoroaster, Pythagoras, Nollius, Alfid, Salmanazer, Epicharmus, Eelen, Avicebron, Empedocles, Abraham, Cebes, Enoch, Ollo Puen, Euripides, Elias, Avicen, Plato, Avenrois, Xistus, Ezekiel, Trismigist, Herviscus, Lactantius, Euclid, Philo, Ireneus, Virgill, Clemens, Marcus Cicero, Tertullian, S. Ambrose, Plotinus, S. Austin, Bocatus, Theophrastus, Plotinus, Jamblicus, Proclus, Beda, Bothius, Psellus, Cardanus, Diodorus, Philostratus, Zamolxis, Origen, Georgius Venetu, Synesius, Severinus, Cornelius Agrippa, Paracelsus, Ryverius, Sennertus, Phroates, Jarchas, L. Verulam, D. Gregory, D. Flood, Doctor Barlow, Des Cartes, R. Lully, Fernelius, Sir Christopher Heydon, Ficinus,

The Postscript.

nus, Agricola, *Mr. Hobbs, Mr. John Gadbury, Eugenius, and Mr. Vincent Wing, Dr. Brown, Mr. Collins, Mr. Moor*, *and many other Antient and Modern Writers, which would be too long to recite: I could prove all I have written to be true by ten thousand witnesses, and the Bible; but I am not bound to give any man so much satisfaction. Thus far I have been free to assist those that understand me, and it is more then I promised; I am in the humour to do my Native Country service, having seen* Spain, Italy, Turky, *and* Greece, *and their learning; but folly in* France *is their highest wisdome, and I cannot find a discreetly moral man amongst them; and from thence we have nothing but fellows that root here in* England, *to the prejudice of Trade, and imployment of our Natives; for several, as* Mounsieur D. &c. *and such Extortioners that creep among women for the sale of Silks and Taffaties, Ribands, Hats,* &c. *get great riches, to the ruine of the Englishmen: I know the King will observe how our Citizens are destroyed by them, his Sacred Majesty sees how they vend vile commodities, and cheat the poor people: Nay, they are the basest of Nations, and therefore not in our harmony, but I have set all into good order, in* the Idea of the Law and Government; *and to make Kingdomes happy, observe those maxims in* my Fundamental Elements of Moral Phylosophy, Policy,

S 3

The Postscript.

licy, Government, and the Lawes.

Many Errours the Compositer hath committed, but the Vertuosi *and* Litterati, *have Apologized (for mine) and the Printers mistakes, which through haste, or other infirmities, were committed: So now let the cowardly counsels of under-wits, and* Lilly, *pass amongst Asses unregarded:* God hath set all in Heaven and Earth into Harmony (except the Devil and Rebels) *for there is a Harmony between* Christ and King Charles, *between the* Angels in Heaven, *and the* Bishops in England; *between the* Saints in Heaven, *and the* Kings Loyal Subjects; *for the King and Bishops command and teach the same Laws of God upon Earth, as God teaches his Saints, Angels, and them, from Heaven: I pray God direct us in this right way, to his glory.*

I know the world will be ready to boy *me out of countenance for this, because my years are few and green, I want their two* Crutches, *the pretended modern* Sanctity, *and that solemnity of the* Beard, *which makes up a* Doctor: *But Gentlemen, in the* Physical *part of this Book, let me advise you, if by what is here written you attain to any knowledge in* Rosie Crucian Medicines, *(by divine assistance) let me advise you, I say, not to attempt any thing rashly. There is in the* Rosie Crucian Records *a memorable story of*

The Postscript.

a Jew, who having by permission rifled some spiritual treasures, was translated in Solitudines, and is kept there for an example to others: I will give you the best counsel that I can, serve God, and honour the King, pray for the Bishops, and their godly able Ministers, do wrong to no man, &c. but do good for evil to all. I will now withdraw, and leave the Stage to the next Actor.

God save the King.

www.ingramcontent.com/pod-product-compliance
Lightning Source LLC
Chambersburg PA
CBHW032049220426
43664CB00008B/924